Ian McEwan's *Atonement*

Also available from Continuum:

Also available in the series

· IAN McEWAN'S

Atonement

JULIE ELLAM

continuum

Continuum

The Tower Building   80 Maiden Lane, Suite 704
11 York Road   New York
London SE1 7NX   NY 10038

www.continuumbooks.com

British Library Cataloguing-in-Publication Data
A catalogue record for this book is available from the British Library.

ISBN: 978-0-8264-4538-4 (Paperback)

Library of Congress Cataloging-in-Publication Data
A catalog record for this book is available from the Library of Congress.

Typeset by YHT Ltd
Printed and bound in Great Britain by the MPG Books Group

Contents

The Novelist

Ian McEwan has had a long and successful writing career that dates from the mid-1970s. Since then, he has gone on to prove his versatility and although he is mainly known as a novelist and writer of short stories, he has also written two librettos, *Or Shall We Die?* (1983) and *For You* (2008), and the film scripts *The Ploughman's Lunch* (1985) and *Soursweet* (1988), which is based on the Timothy Mo novel. *The Daydreamer* (1994) is a work of children's fiction.

He has become a mainstay in British contemporary literature and each new publication is largely welcomed by the critics and his expanding readership. His fiction has become known for its displays of meticulous research and his novels are recognizable, especially since the late 1990s, for an economy of style. From the outset he was seen as a promising new talent and with his first publication, a collection of short stories entitled *First Love, Last Rites* (1975), he received a Somerset Maugham Award. His second work, *In Between the Sheets* (1978), which is another collection of short fiction, has a similar thematic use of violence while also maintaining a distance from its subject matter. Over the decades, his writing has been less willing to shock and he has evolved gradually into a writer with broad appeal. It is also of note that his novels are studied more at A-level than works by any other living British novelist (Mullan, 2007).

His work was highly regarded before the publication of *Atonement* (2001a), but this particular novel continues to stand out as one of his greatest achievements to date and is an exaggerated testament to how he is a rarity in the literary establishment. That is, *Atonement* highlights how he is both celebrated as a writer of literary fiction and also massively popular with the reading public. Since its original publication, it has been on national and international bestselling lists and has sold four million copies, which, again, is an unusual feat for a work of this type. The adaptation to film in 2007 has served to contribute to the novel's high profile. It has brought about a further resurgence in sales and was republished as a tie-in with the film.

McEwan was born in 1948 in Aldershot and spent the early part of his childhood abroad according to where his father was posted by the army. In an interview with Kate Kellaway, he refers to how he 'grew up with the "detritus of war" around him' (Kellaway, 2001). He belongs to the generation that grew up immediately after the war and it was made a part of his life with the stories his father told him of his involvement in it and with the fact that his babysitters were corporals. This is significant in relation to *Atonement* given that his father used to tell him about what happened to him in the Dunkirk retreat.

From 1959 to 1966, he attended Woolverstone Hall, a state boarding school in Suffolk, and this is described by Matthew Kibble in *Literature Online* as a place where 'working-class children from central London were taught alongside those who, like himself, came from military families', and is a former school of writers such as Rudyard Kipling (Kibble, 2000). McEwan is quoted in John Mullan's 'Profile' as saying he looks back at himself at this time as being 'sort of depressed' and 'more or less obedient' to the requirements of studying for his exams up to degree level. He reasons that this is understandable when one considers that his parents were 2,000 miles away in North Africa at the time. He says that his early fiction showed a 'bold' and perhaps too violent side that, he implies, was an outlet for the more introverted aspect of his personality in these younger days (Mullan, 2007). He is also on record as saying that he did not weep when he attended boarding school, but 'just clammed up for four or five years' (Deveney, 2005).

He went on to study English and French at Sussex University from 1967 to 1970. His parents were working class and both left school at the age of 14, and in an interview with Catherine Deveney in the *New Scotsman* he tells how proud his father was that his son went on to study at university. He sees his parents' generation as a 'wasted' one, in that although his father was intelligent he was inevitably unable to go to university because of the need to earn a living (Deveney, 2005).

When tracing McEwan's background to explain his success, his decision to take the then new MA in Modern Fiction and Creative Writing at the University of East Anglia (1970–1971) appears to be one of those pivotal moments that he favours so often in his work. The MA, which was founded by Professor Malcolm Bradbury and Sir Angus Wilson, has since been recognized as influential for many others, such as Kazuo Ishiguro, Anne Enright and Tracy Chevalier, but McEwan was the first: 'The significance of the Wilson-Bradbury connection, in a broader literary-historical sense, is that McEwan comes out of a literary stable (so to speak), associated with the liberal identity in crisis' (Head, 2007, p. 4). This point is proven plainly in his early fiction and with more confidence and complexity in later novels such as *Enduring Love* (1997), *Atonement* and *Saturday* (2005).

Dominic Head gives further biographical details of this period and outlines how in 1972 McEwan joined the hippie trail to Afghanistan. In 1974, he moved to Stockwell from Norwich and became involved with the *New Review*, which became a magnet for other emerging writers such as Martin Amis, Julian Barnes and Craig Raine. At this time, he was also awaiting the publication of *First Love, Last Rites* and working on *In Between the Sheets* in pursuit of a writing career (Head, 2007, p. 4).

Early fiction

McEwan's writing career from this period into the 1980s is significant because of the use of violence, obscenity and taboo-breaking subject matter. Morality is twisted or rejected, as in the story 'Homemade', which is included in *First Love, Last Rites* and was his first publication after being accepted by *The New American Review*. This is where the adolescent first-person narrator decides to lose his virginity by raping his 10-year-old sister, Connie, and the story begins at the end with her crying. It goes on to detail how he learns to become an adult with Raymond, who is a year older, and begins to think of his virginity as a 'malodorous albatross' (McEwan, 1991, p. 29). This chilling tale succeeds in being as shocking and disturbing as appears to have been intended.

The eponymous short story, 'First Love, Last Rites', is set over the period of a summer and is also preoccupied with the development from adolescence into adulthood. The first-person narrator and his girlfriend, Sissel, hear noises behind the skirting board and the last rites refer to the death of the rat that they have heard, which the narrator refers to as 'our familiar', as well as the end of their youth (McEwan, 1991, p. 96).

McEwan's first novel, *The Cement Garden* (1978), is an unsettling take on family life and culminates in sibling incest after the four children are orphaned. When they are left alone, their circle tightens in a harsh parody of the institution of the family and it is only disrupted by the outsider, Derek. In McEwan's interview with Deveney, he explains how this novel is about 'absent parents'. He also says how it addresses the sentiments he had while growing up in which he wished his parents would 'somehow painlessly melt away' as this would leave the 'ground cleared' for him (Deveney, 2005). This daydream echoes the Freudian formulation of the family romance, where the child imagines being free of his or her parents, and is connected to the process of growing up and separating from the once idealized parents. The orphaned child has been a significant figure in literature as he or she is then given a freedom and independence from parental (and societal) control.

The Comfort of Strangers (1981) is his second novel and is set in an unnamed city that can only be Venice. The narrative follows two tourists, Colin and Mary, as they become caught up in a relationship with Robert and Caroline. Just as *The Cement Garden* refuses to offer a traditionally moral perspective of the family, *The Comfort of Strangers* destabilizes the truism of a loving relationship as it represents sado-masochism rather than dismisses it. Because it refuses to simply criticize violence it is an unsettling work, as the concept of collusion in the perpetration of violent acts is placed in the foreground (again) and the readers are entrusted to evaluate if it is possible to be complicit as a victim. In terms of questions of

morality this is a problematic debate, as there is the implication
that there is a choice taken in being a victim, and also the suggestion that it is possible to take pleasure from this too.

By engaging with taboo subjects such as incest and sado-
masochism rather than only condemning them, McEwan has
earned the reputation of a controversial writer, and in the past has
been known by the moniker 'Ian Macabre' and as an *enfant terrible*
of contemporary British writing (Kellaway, 2001). Some may say
this view was confirmed in 1979 when the production of *Solid
Geometry* (which he adapted from a story taken from *First Love, Last
Rites*) was halted by the BBC on the grounds of obscenity. The
storage of a penis in a jar is the standard cited reason for this
censorship, but, as Kiernan Ryan points out, the smashing of the jar
and the obvious ineffectuality of the member is also an allegory for
questioning patriarchal dominance (Ryan, 1994, p.29). The
screenplay was later published in *The Imitation Game: Three Plays for
Television* (1981) and refilmed and screened on Channel 4 in 2002.
Ryan regards the adaptation as significant when looking back over
McEwan's early career: '*Solid Geometry* emerges with hindsight as a
kind of bridge between McEwan's first three books and the new
territories mapped in *The Imitation Game*' (Ryan, 1994, p. 27). He
goes on to imply that this play version highlights a movement
towards demonstrating an interest in feminism, and possesses a
wider understanding of sexual politics than has previously been
seen in McEwan's writing.

Of his next main novels, there is a continued examination of the
effects of horrific incidents on the main protagonists, as well as an
increase in confidence in his storytelling techniques. In *The Child in
Time* (1987), for instance, Stephen and his wife are observed as
they suffer the grief that comes with the abduction of their child.
Irony is also heaped on as Stephen is an accidentally successful

children's author and a member of the Official Commission on Child Care.

The Innocent (1990), which is set in Berlin in the 1950s during the Cold War, is both a thriller and love story. The idea of the loss of innocence is a central concern and this is examined through its central protagonist, Leonard Marnham. *Black Dogs* (1992) remembers the lasting effects of the Second World War through the horror generated by the eponymous dogs and also returns to Berlin after the wall comes down. This was followed by *Enduring Love*, which begins momentously with a tragedy involving a hot-air balloon and goes on to cover the theme of obsession most notably when Jed Parry stalks Joe Rose. Science is another key theme, and this is made central because of Joe's work as a populist science writer.

The Booker Prize-winner *Amsterdam* (1998), which beat off other contenders such as *Master Georgie* (1998) by Beryl Bainbridge and *Breakfast on Pluto* (1998) by Patrick McCabe, begins with the funeral of Molly Lane and introduces three of her former lovers. The underlying theme of euthanasia is brought in at this early stage and provides the means for the final element of black comedy. It is commonly thought by critics that this is one of McEwan's weaker novels and has been regarded, therefore, as an unlikely one to win the Booker (Lyall, 1998). Both *The Comfort of Strangers* and *Black Dogs* were shortlisted in previous years, and it has been touted that McEwan was given the prize for *Amsterdam* as a consolation.

More recent fiction

Since then, *Atonement*, *Saturday* and *On Chesil Beach* (2007) have also been shortlisted for this award, and McEwan has been named twice as a contender for the Man Booker International Prize (in 2005 and 2007). He has also been the recipient of numerous other awards, such as the National Book Critics' Circle Award in 2003 for *Atonement* and the Whitbread Novel Award for *The Child in Time*. As if to confirm his stature as a highly thought of British author, and perhaps to confirm his place in the establishment now, he was also awarded the CBE in 2000.

Over the decades, his writing has moved from placing a covert rather than overt psychological pressure on his characters and readers. In 1994, Ryan argued the case that claims of a vast change in McEwan's writing should only be made cautiously: 'The focus of McEwan's did shift dramatically after *The Imitation Game*. But the temptation to reduce his development to an exemplary tale of moral maturation or artistic depletion needs to be resisted. Such simplified accounts of his trajectory obscure the continuities and contradictions of his work' (Ryan, 1994, p. 4).

Following Ryan's reasoning, a sweeping account of his *oeuvre* would only be detrimental to the individuality of each of his works, but one only needs to compare *Atonement*, *Saturday* or *On Chesil Beach* with *The Cement Garden* to see a more developed use of characterization and intricacy of structure in each of these later works. It is also necessary to remember that Ryan's point was made in the early 1990s and so he did not have the luxury of seeing the considerable change in McEwan's later style. It is not that his earlier writing was immature, but the point stands that a desire to please with more complexity has taken over from the desire to shock, and this is evident when considering his trajectory. McEwan states in 'The Ghost in My Family' that his 'heart sinks' at what he now calls his 'staring-at-the-wall fiction' and now wants to create a 'realised world' (Appleyard, 2007). At this point, he says he feels he has greater clarity as a writer than he did in the 1970s and is more able to expand on his ideas. This gradual shift in perspectives has come about with a more ambitious view of the possibilities available. *On Chesil Beach*, for example, is a pared-down tale of a doomed marriage that does not survive the honeymoon, and although it retains some of the now-familiar McEwan bleak worldview as well as looking at the effects of a single, momentous action, its style is elevated from his earlier work.

Atonement is less willing to challenge taboos than his earlier novels, but it still maintains the same overhanging threat that has been a consistent feature over the years. In 'A Version of Events', Robert MacFarlane explains how because of this it is still recognizably McEwan's: 'While the explicit morbidity of, say, *In Between the Sheets* (1978) or *The Cement Garden* (1978) has receded in his more recent work, the air of imminent calamity remains. This is powerfully the case in the opening part of *Atonement*.' This long opening first section maintains the idea of impending catastrophe because, as MacFarlane argues, the narrative patiently stays with the long, hot summer day in 1935 until Briony commits her crime (MacFarlane, 2001, p. 23).

This comes when Briony falsely accuses Robbie of raping her cousin, Lola, and is the trigger for the events that follow. Atoning for this sin becomes the ostensible purpose behind writing the novel and the reason for the title. The exploration of the consequences that ensue after one life-changing event is a common feature in McEwan's work and this has been memorably evoked in *Enduring Love*, for example, when the freak accident involving the hot-air balloon leads to an entanglement between the survivors. In

Atonement, Briony's accusation and decision to stay firm to it are at the centre as Part One leads the readers with deliberation to the time she commits her crime.

Although a relatively low-profile writer, McEwan has occasionally been brought into the media spotlight and asked to share his own life-changing events with the reading public. The idea that the pivotal, key scenes occur in his biography as well as his writing has been noted by Bryan Appleyard in interview with him in 'The Ghost in My Family'. Appleyard also uses this opportunity to discuss a connection between the life of the writer and his art. He makes specific references to the time in 2002 when McEwan discovered he had a full brother, David, who had been adopted in 1942. Their parents had him adopted in an attempt to cover up their affair, as this was before the death of their mother's first husband in 1944. Appleyard also offers an uncanny understanding of McEwan in his explanation of the discovery of his brother. 'McEwan tells me the tale freely though hesitantly as if he is struggling to turn it into one of his own stories. Yet I feel an eerie sense that somehow his fiction has retrospectively created his life. Whenever he is in the news for not strictly literary reasons, the stories always seem to have a dark, McEwanish colouring' (Appleyard, 2007).

There are always difficulties when making connections between an author's life and his or her fiction, primarily because there is the danger of conflating the two and simplifying both narratives. As this chapter is concerned with the novelist, though, it is necessary to introduce some background details to McEwan's life such as this revelation about his brother. He has also been reported as being involved in a lengthy divorce and custody battle with his first wife, Penny Allen, and Kellaway points out that in the late 1990s the news of the conflict between them overshadowed his writing career: 'For since McEwan won the Booker Prize in 1998 with *Amsterdam*, the fight over the custody of his sons has earned him even more publicity than his professional success' (Kellaway, 2001). He was finally awarded custody after repeated visits to court and, as Kellaway argues, it would have been understandable if there had been no more novels. For one who is generally reluctant to discuss his private life in the public arena, he is drawn out in this interview to explain how he continued writing during and after this period. His reasoning is simply that the division between writing and the family has to be overcome, and *Atonement* is the novel that came out of this period.

He has also stated that after having children he felt he could not return to the same themes he used in *The Child in Time*. This shift in interest may be a signifier of his change in perspective, or a heightened sense of maturity; it is not necessarily an indication of encroaching conservatism. In *Saturday*, for example, Henry Perowne may be seen to reflect aspects of McEwan's views about the war in Iraq and is reactionary in his fear of attack from outside forces, but he is not a mouthpiece for McEwan as, again, this is a work of fiction.

Whatever the reasons for this move to a more secure or even stifled world, John Banville's review of *Saturday* is damning for what he perceives as relative narrowness despite McEwan being inspired by 9/11, and is nostalgic for the earlier McEwan incarnations that took perverse delight in the discomfort of others. Banville has argued since in the documentary *Being John Banville* (2008) that he was being critical of the fawning critics rather than McEwan, but does say in the review that McEwan is showing 'a disturbing tendency towards mellowness' of late and wonders if the decision by Perowne's son Theo to think small may also be the 'motto' of this work (Banville, 2005).

For McEwan fans this may seem harsh, but it remains a useful balance against the at times unquestioning adoration, as is demonstrated in Appleyard's conclusion: 'T. S. Eliot once said that the great writer achieves the critical language in which he is to be understood. That is precisely what McEwan has achieved. But in a sense he has gone even further. For why does the story of David carry such resonance and poignancy? Because his understanding of our world, of what we take seriously, of what ultimately matters, has infected us all. We are what McEwan's mirror reflects, uncertain creatures yearning for atonement' (Appleyard, 2007).

To return to the McEwan biography, as well as the infamous divorce case and the discovery of his brother, he was also the focus of a controversy when plagiarism charges were aimed at him for *Atonement* in 2006 for drawing on Lucilla Andrews' *No Time for Romance* (1977). Appleyard explains how each of these personal stories has been regarded as newsworthy, and that the interest shown is explicable because of his standing in the public realm rather than being attempts to revile him: 'It was a particularly cretinous charge since McEwan had acknowledged Andrews in the book and all novelists, particularly when writing historically, must use some nonfiction sources. But the prominence given to all three stories – the brother, the divorce and the plagiarism charge – are all evidence of McEwan's stature in the national imagination. Increasingly he is seen as our national writer' (Appleyard, 2007). Although generalizing, this claim has some weight as McEwan still resists demonization, despite the high profile, and still tends to be understood through his fiction rather than his biography.

This charge of plagiarism brought other authors out in defence of the practice of using contemporary documents to help substantiate historical novels. Nigel Reynolds in the *Telegraph* reports how Margaret Atwood and Thomas Keneally are among those who offered their support against the criticism and Thomas Pynchon argued in favour of the necessity of being able to turn to other artefacts: 'Unless we were actually there we must turn to people who were, or to letters, contemporary reporting, the encyclopaedia, the internet, until, with luck at some point we can begin to make things up on our own' (Reynolds, 2006). This amounts to not just a defence of the writing of historical novels, but also of the writing of fiction, as this art blurs the boundaries between truth and lies, and fact and fiction.

Literary influences, contexts and the writing process

On his arrival on the literary scene in the early 1970s, McEwan came to be seen as part of a new generation of British novelists. Along with writers such as Martin Amis, Salman Rushdie and Julian Barnes, his emergence helped bring about a renaissance of sorts in contemporary British fiction and this was later confirmed in his inclusion on *Granta*'s prescient list of Best of Young British Novelists in 1983. To assess these then-upcoming writers, it is of use to look to what came before and see why these were considered such vibrant talents. Stephen Moss remarks how they were viewed as comparatively bold and modern and argues that in this period there was a 'huge appetite for change' (Moss, 2001). These latest literary novelists that looked to contemporary Britain filled a vacuum that was at least partially recognized by *Granta*. Robert McCrum harks back to the 1970 Booker Prize winner (Bernice Rubens) and shortlisted writers (Al Barker, Elizabeth Bowen, Iris Murdoch and William Trevor) to make his point that at this time, when McEwan was in his early 20s, 'the house of English fiction looked like a shabby, suburban Edwardian rectory'. McCrum also shows how McEwan was part of the next generation to stake his claim on this 'house': 'Young Ian McEwan was well-placed to break a few windows and establish squatters' rights.' He sees him as being 'well-placed' at least partly because 'he was both part of post-imperial Britain, and outside it' in the time he spent abroad when his father was serving in the army and in his education (McCrum, 2005, p. 5).

Moss argues how these writers have since become 'the literary old guard', as there are few rivals appearing to succeed them: 'Amis, Rushdie, McEwan and Barnes are our modern canon, but the canonization has a singular contemporary feel: increasingly, we know more about their lives, loves, fights – even their teeth – than their work. They have become the Great Writers we have to read about; reading what they write appears to be optional' (Moss, 2001). It is also possible that their influence remains strong due to merit as well as lack of opposition.

Although known as a novelist and, as Moss states, for some of his biographical detail, McEwan has also inserted himself in the public consciousness as one who is prepared to move beyond fiction in his essays and articles. As well as having a background in literature, he has also expressed an ongoing interest in science and science writing. His research for several novels, including *Saturday* and *Amsterdam*, makes this evident. When asked by David Lynn about the writers he most admires, he refers to *Creation* (2006) by the American biologist E. O. Wilson and explains that he sees this as putting 'a hand out across the divide' between science and religion. In this interview, he also eschews aspects of relativism in postmodern criticism and says that plagiarists, when claiming events that have happened to others as one's own, should be 'named and shamed'. He also warns against drifting away 'in a cloud of unknown relativism' (Lynn, 2007).

In 'A Parallel Tradition', which is an expanded essay of a talk given by McEwan at the London School of Economics to celebrate the 30th anniversary of Richard Dawkins' *The Selfish Gene* (1976), he extrapolates on the pleasures it is possible to take in the reading of science writing and its search for truth (McEwan, 2006a). This sits at angles with the use of postmodern influences, and perhaps demonstrates that he has reservations about being overwhelmed by any particular movement or stance.

McEwan has also been vocal in expressing his views beyond literature into politics and has broached the subject of terrorism. In the more distant past, he also has been an opponent of the nuclear arms race. By choosing to lay bare his views, he also found controversy in 2008 when defending Martin Amis from criticisms of being racist. In *Corriere della Sera*, McEwan entered the debate to defend Amis most notably against the *Guardian* and said that he despises 'Islamism' and argued in favour of Amis's right to challenge fundamentalism (Cohen, 2008). Whatever one's view of his politics may be, and they are visibly Eurocentric in their concerns, his outspokenness beyond the role of publicizing his novels means that he belongs to the older tradition of the novelist prepared to use his or her literary fame to publicly discuss contemporary politics. This has also been seen in his article 'Only Love and Then Oblivion', which came out soon after the 9/11 attacks on the World Trade Center. Here, he discusses empathy and attempts to imagine the experience of being on board one of the hijacked planes: 'Imagining what it is like to be someone other than yourself is at the core of our humanity. It is the essence of compassion, and is the beginning of morality' (McEwan, 2001c).

Just as a shift in his writing is traceable, so the influences on his work have varied in intensity during the course of his professional writing career. His early style, for example, is often regarded as being indebted to existentialist thinking in that it takes a thematic distance from traditional morality. As a literary novel that relishes the pleasure in being self-aware about its fictionality, *Atonement* also reveals its many influences. The epigraph, which is taken from Jane Austen's *Northanger Abbey* (1818), is an ironic declaration to the reader to be wary of the literary imagination and is also a taster of how in the writing of it, McEwan called it 'my Jane Austen novel, my country house novel, my one-hot-day novel' (Kellaway, 2001). The Jane Austen references at first sit lightly, especially considering his earlier novels, but this is also an apt label. The country house setting, the subtle challenge to class difference and above all the ironic depiction of the dangers of the literary imagination confirm this tag.

As if in confirmation of this, McEwan explains the influence of nineteenth-century writings on his work in an interview with Lynn. While indicating how *Atonement* could not have been written 'without all the experiments in fiction and reflections on point of view' and, by default, the movements of modernism and post-modernism, he argues how we also should not turn away from 'the notion of character' and how the nineteenth century 'formalized' this. He refers to Austen, Honoré de Balzac, Charles Dickens and Gustave Flaubert as examples of earlier authors who have taught us to expect to look into the minds of others (Lynn, 2007).

In 'Ian McEwan: Contemporary Realism and the Novel of Ideas', Judith Seaboyer claims that his novels demonstrate both aspects of reformist politics and strongly observed details of its contemporary subjects. She uses this template to compare his work to that of George Eliot and Virginia Woolf respectively (Seaboyer, 2005, p. 23). She marks a shift in his work from *The Comfort of Strangers* onwards as she sees this as his first 'novel of ideas'. She considers this to be a gothic text that looks into the psychology of fear as well as marking his 'transitional shift towards a traditional realism in which the private sphere is not only mirrored in that of the public but is a way of addressing broader social issues' (Seaboyer, 2005, p. 24). She finishes this chapter by arguing that his use of realism in later novels, including *Atonement*, continues to make the readers puzzle over how to live the ethical life: 'As we have seen, McEwan's realism holds up a nicely polished mirror to show us reality, but with *Atonement* he allows us to experience the ethics of writing and reading that reality' (Seaboyer, 2005, p. 32).

As McEwan has said, it is no longer possible to trust the omniscient point of view, and a bridge between here and the nineteenth-century novel is found in Woolf's work and, as Seaboyer stresses, it is possible to point to the influence she has on his writing. It is most evident in *Atonement* when she looms over Briony's decision to become a recognized writer as she matures. Woolf is also openly referred to in Briony's reading of *The Waves* (1931) and in the short story she sends to *Horizon*. With more subtlety, echoes of Woolf's style appear in Chapter 6 of Part One when Emily Tallis lies in bed with a migraine as she listens to the movements in the house.

The engagement with postmodernism is apparent in the decision to remove the possibility of closure in the final section and in the way it is highlighted throughout that this is a work of fiction. Closure is refused in that the first version of Robbie and Cecilia being united in Part Three is undermined by Briony in 'London, 1999'. Briony also emphasizes here how this is a work of fiction, and consequently drags the readers out of the realist dream and reminds them that the author is deciding the outcomes. By highlighting its fictionality in this way, *Atonement* becomes another novel that exposes the role of the novelist while challenging readers' expectations.

Comparisons may be made with works such as *The French Lieutenant's Woman* (1969) by John Fowles in that this played with and deconstructed the format of the realist nineteenth-century novel to the point that the readers were left to choose which ending they preferred. Geoff Dyer's review argues that there is a further overlap between the two: 'While John Fowles was working on *The French Lieutenant's Woman*, he reminded himself that this was not a book that one of the Victorian novelists forgot to write but, perhaps, one that they had failed to write. A similar impulse underwrites *Atonement*. It is less about a novelist harking nostalgically back to the consoling uncertainties of the past than it is about creatively extending and hauling a defining part of the British literary tradition up to and into the twenty-first century' (Dyer, 2001).

By revealing its fictionality with subtlety in Part One and unremittingly in 'London, 1999', the nod to postmodernism is made. The layering of numerous intertexts and references to other works is also an aspect of this as echoes of other novels reverberate. This is exemplified by Kellaway when she describes Briony as belonging to 'one of a select band of children' in literary history: 'Like Maisie in Henry James's *What Maisie Knew* or Leo in L. P. Hartley's *The Go-Between*, Briony is a child who becomes implicated in an adult sexual relationship she does not understand' (Kellaway, 2001).

Largely because of the Dunkirk section, which is Part Two, and the descriptions of the treatment of the wounded in Part Three, this novel also belongs to the genre of war literature. It feeds the appetite for stories of war that have been returned to intermittently by British authors in the late twentieth and early twenty-first centuries, as with the First World War-inspired *Birdsong* (1993) by Sebastian Faulks and the *Regeneration* trilogy by Pat Barker. More specifically, the Second World War is the backdrop for *Spies* (2002) by Michael Frayn, which also draws on an adult's perspective of childhood.

Knowledge of the craft of writing also underpins McEwan's success and apart from the many distinct literary intertexts that he uses and the in-depth research he undertakes, his imagination, needless to say, also plays a part in his success. In his interview with Lynn, he explains his practice of writing and the pleasure he takes in unexpected ideas that come through in the process: 'Sometimes I have to trick myself into doing things. But I do see writing, the actual physical matter of writing, as an act of imagination. And the best days, the best mornings are the ones in which forcing down a sentence may generate a surprise. A combination of ideas, or simply a noun meeting an adjective that suddenly gives me pleasure. Whole characters have sometimes emerged for me simply out of a sentence' (Lynn, 2007). He refers to the unplanned appearance of Nettle and Mace in Part Two of *Atonement* as an example of this.

The esteem held for McEwan's writing is seen repeatedly in the high sales figures and mainly positive reviews, and for now he is one of the remaining darlings of his generation of promising new talent of the 1970s and 1980s. He has secured this position as the focus of his work has moved over the decades from the brutal to the disquieting. This has come about while he continues to demonstrate the same penchant for menace that appeared in his first collection of short stories.

2

The Novel

Atonement has come to be regarded as one of McEwan's finest works and is tentatively seen as a modern classic, but such terms are easy to say and less easy to qualify. This chapter analyses the structure, main themes and characterization, to unravel its complexity and to explore the reasons behind its popularity. The use of metaphors and narrative devices are similarly examined so that his technical skill can be discussed in more detail. In addition, references are made to its literary quality and this includes an appreciation of the influences of realism, modernism and postmodernism.

When taking an overview of how the novel holds together, the tone and style become all the more significant in that the narrative refuses to fully draw the reader in. This effect climaxes in 'London, 1999', but as Colm Tóibín argues in his review of *On Chesil Beach*, both this and *Atonement* deliberately hold the reader at bay: 'The writing also shares the almost stilted diction of McEwan's novel *Atonement*, a diction used with immense care to create distance and irony, without creating too much of either. It is like putting just enough air in a hot air balloon to allow it to fly, making sure, however, that it can land as well' (Tóibín, 2007, p. 29). The allusion to the hot-air balloon brings *Enduring Love* into the frame of reference while also outlining a now consistent technique of being able to keep the attention of the readers, as it also refuses to be a populist text. As well as finding a convergence with other McEwan works, *Atonement* also stands apart from them as the telling of the story is made as imperative as the story that is being told. This has the familiar trademarks, in the use of the pivotal moment, distancing techniques and the build-up of menace, but it may be differentiated from its predecessors and many other contemporary novels for its assured grace.

Structure and content

At first glance, this has a simple structure of three main sections and a conclusion of sorts in the shorter fourth part ('London, 1999'). On the surface, these first three sections may be labelled as covering one hot day in 1935 in the Tallis country home, a close-up of the retreat of the Allied soldiers at Dunkirk, and then an exploration of the duties involved in wartime nursing. The final shift to 1999 gives the novel a span of over 60 years, but the main narrative revolves around the Second World War and the years before it. As a whole, this is ambitious in its breadth and has an intricacy that belies its first reading.

It is not revealed until the end of Part Three that this novel has been written by Briony, as is made evident with her initials B. T. and the date 1999. With this news, it follows that all that has been read before must be re-assessed, as we are now led to believe that it has been influenced by Briony's perspective. It is also explained in 'London, 1999' that this is her attempt to atone for lying about Robbie raping Lola and has unified the lovers – Cecilia and Robbie – in fiction only, and so it is not until the second reading that one is able to recognize fully how central Briony is to the way the narrative has unfolded. This information must, therefore, be remembered in any analysis of this work. Part One is a relatively slower-paced realist narrative that shifts from the point of view of one character to another as it leads up to the moment when Robbie is arrested for a crime he did not commit. It is only in hindsight, after Briony's revelation that this is her work, that the apparently distant third person of Part One is seen to be crafted from her subjective perspective. This is also when we understand that she has assumed the perspectives of others while claiming to make reparations for the sin of lying.

Just as Tóibín highlights the connection between this and other McEwan novels, Claire Messud points out the resemblance between *Atonement* and *Black Dogs* as the latter is also 'a tale told in retrospect, and convolutedly, through the intermediary of the narrator, Jeremy, son-in-law of the Tremaines' (Messud, 2002). In *Atonement*, though, the discovery that Briony has been ordering events is one that entirely challenges the readers' understanding of what has come before.

Through Briony, McEwan alerts the readers to not trust the author (be that him or Briony) as well as warning of the dangers of the literary imagination. The following reference is one of the most significant of the novel, as it forces the readers to recall that we are reading a fiction, and is a remarkable use of irony if we remember the surprise is delivered by a fictional character: 'It is only in this last version that my lovers end well, standing side by side on a South London pavement as I walk away. All the preceding drafts were pitiless. But now I can no longer think what purpose would be served if, say, I tried to persuade my reader, by direct or indirect means, that Robbie Turner died of septicaemia at Bray Dunes on 1 June 1940, or that Cecilia was killed in September of the same year by the bomb that destroyed Balham Underground Station' (p. 370). It is also ironic that Briony claims to not see the purpose of revealing that Robbie died at Dunkirk and Cecilia at Balham, but does so anyway, and it seems as though she cannot resist a final manipulation of the readers' expectations.

Part One

The long summer's day in 1935 that constitutes Part One, which is divided into 14 chapters, is an exercise in explanation of and, at times, a subtle excuse for Briony's actions. In retrospect, the clues that this is her work are set out for us, as when it is reiterated how at just 13 she has a precocious love of writing and order. As stated, it includes familiar aspects of other work by McEwan in that the slow pace allows the underlying menace to develop as the scenes shift between the points of view of different characters as Briony is seen to imagine them. This is mainly brought about by the movement between the perspectives of these characters as they view the same scene and, because of this, Part One has the effect of grinding slowly towards Robbie's arrest. This inhabiting of the minds of the different characters also exemplifies McEwan's professed interest in the use of characterization in nineteenth-century novels and in how such works give the readers the opportunity to enter the minds of the principal figures (Lynn, 2007). He endows Briony the writer with the same ability that he admires, and uses his version of Cyril Connolly to teach her to avoid leaning so heavily on modernist techniques (in the guise of Woolf) (p. 312).

A comparison between chapters 2 and 3 exemplifies this use of shifting point of view. Cecilia and Briony are used respectively to reveal their separate interpretations of what happens when Cecilia and Robbie are at the fountain together and struggle over the vase. From the vantage point of the window, Briony imagines he is proposing to Cecilia and then sees him raise his hand and understands this to mean he is ordering her to obey him. She comes to recognize that this is not a fairytale and has instead glimpsed the adult world, but overriding all these emotions is the desire to write.

The atmosphere of developing tension should be evident to readers familiar with McEwan's other novels as this has been his stock-in-trade. For the newcomers, it may be initially less easy to spot, but occurs in the deliberately slow pace and in the stream of references to the heat of this long day. The heat wave is described as oppressive and cloying, and is made central in Chapter 9, for example, when Emily tells Betty to prepare a salad instead of the roast she had previously requested. Betty's reaction embodies her frustration with the temperature as well as with her employer. The pressure that is emphasized by the weather is also apparent in Emily's thoughts as she tries to avoid having a migraine in Chapter 6: 'She thought of the vast heat that rose above the house and park, and lay across the Home Counties like smoke, suffocating the farms and towns, and she thought of the baking railway tracks that were bringing Leon and his friend, and the roasting black-roofed carriage in which they would sit by an open window' (p. 64).

This lengthy first section also allows for space to be given to observe and critique the landscape of a pre-war, upper middle-class England on a microscale. The range in class differences between the servants, their families and the Tallises are elemental to the plot as these allow for tensions to be expressed. The snobbery imbued in the characterization of Emily and Leon in particular means that the contrast between the hierarchies is sharpened. The supposed grandeur of the country home, which is as flawed as the family who owns it, is, therefore, an apt background for deconstructing the privileged status of the upper middle classes. The clenched relationship between the different family members such as Cecilia and Emily, and the reported strain between Emily and Hermione also symbolize how the harmony between the Tallises is only superficial.

The barely disguised annoyance between the gathered family members and associates is introduced in the scene in the kitchen and culminates at the evening meal. This unrest may be read as a figurative reference to the political climate of the period as well as a means for pointing out how dysfunctional this group is. The prospect of war hangs over them and is made specific in Paul Marshall's allusions to the profits he will make with his chocolate bars, and in Jack Tallis's work for 'Eventuality Planning' at the Home Office (p. 122).

This ominous view of the future is dismissed by Emily when she comes across horrifying figures that estimate the huge loss of life if war occurs. This is not only typical of the way she maintains her feminine passivity by evading problems, but is also representative of a *laissez-faire* attitude to the growing threat of fascism in mainland Europe at this time. Philip Tew notes how Emily sees this predicted massive loss of lives of up to five million in the threatened war, and how she readily dismisses this as 'a form of self-aggrandisement' (Tew, 2004, pp. 149–50). This ability to deny unpleasantness, let alone the prospect of genocide, is in keeping with her characterization, and is also written of as a definable quality in others of her ilk. Tew contrasts her view in 1935 with Robbie's experiences in Dunkirk: 'The historical reference cumulatively indicates two kinds of Britain, one before the cataclysms, personal and public, one afterward. Thus McEwan conveys something of the almost anachronistic quality and emotional ill-preparedness of this upper middle-class in an imperial period that it felt might well be an ongoing heyday' (Tew, 2004, p. 169).

Part One ends with the arrest of Robbie and at last the tension of the day reaches a climax. By finishing with this scene, the idyll is forever exposed as being unreal. It also marks the end of an era of relative innocence as Grace Turner shouts 'Liars!' as the police car drives Robbie away (p. 187). When she first stops the car, her outrage is described as the 'final confrontation' and undermines what would have been a 'seamless day' for Briony (p. 186). Grace's actions disrupt her romanticized view of what has been happening, as she records that she had been thinking that Cecilia was watching the car 'tranquilly' as it took Robbie away (p. 186). This romantic interpretation is enhanced by Briony when it is noted that she 'knew she had never loved her sister more than now' (p. 186). Grace's anger gives a contrast to this perspective and also emphasizes Briony's naivety.

Part Two

The lack of chapter divisions in Part Two adds to the disorder of the situation being evoked and enhances the eventual chaos of Robbie's thoughts. This disorder is made all the more apparent because it differs so sharply from the way Part One is organized.

Part Two moves abruptly to what transpires to be the war and more specifically the Dunkirk retreat. The break from the past is described as 'savage' by McEwan, and a different tone and style are used to reflect this dislocation from what has gone before with a sense of immediacy (DVD, 2008). The disruption of the daydream at the country house, where the superficial has been seen to dominate, is first introduced with Grace's anger at the arrest of her son and is ultimately shattered by this shift to the war. There is a lack of initial exposition and it is not until the third page into this section that 'he' is finally introduced as Robbie Turner (and is known as Turner from then on). It begins as Robbie, Nettle and Mace try to find their way back to the coast to return to England and the readers are plunged into their environment: 'There were horrors enough, but it was the unexpected detail that threw him and afterwards would not let him go' (p. 191). His disorientation is matched by the readers as he then looks for his map, wonders where it is and eventually realizes it has been in his left hand for over an hour: 'He had prised it from the fingers of a captain in the West Kents lying in a ditch outside – outside where?' (p. 191). The information about why he is there and how he is still in touch with Cecilia is only leaked out gradually and is related via his memories and the letters she sends him.

Looked at as a whole, this Part shows the fragmentation of civilization and the gradual breakdown of Robbie as he attempts to survive his wound in order to return home. It is described how he finds himself 'in the grip of illogical certainties', as the infection takes hold and those around him lose sense of what is happening. His hallucinatory state is mirrored by what he sees at Bray Dunes when, for example, a lieutenant demands that Nettle tie up his laces even though chaos surrounds them as the area is now the 'terminus' for the 'rout' (p. 247).

As the end of Part Two approaches, Robbie's hallucinations become more vivid and he is increasingly less coherent. Prior to this, his memories were distinct from the present, but as he comes closer to death his regrets overwhelm him: 'Invisible baggage. He must go back and get the boy from the tree. He had done it before. He had gone back where no one else was and found the boys under a tree and carried Pierrot on his shoulders and Jackson in his arms, across the park' (p. 262). He thinks of the boy left behind as 'more unfinished business' and wants to go back to the field and 'ask the Flemish lady and her son if they held him accountable for their deaths. For one can assume too much sometimes, in fits of conceited self-blame' (p. 263). His self-recriminations mix with self-justification as he goes on to think how this 'lady' might say that he carried the twins but not 'us' and also that he is 'not guilty' (p. 263). Yet again, the guilt that he has been tarnished with because of Briony's lie is also seen to infect his thoughts.

His point of view of the time when he was arrested is also given and how Cecilia had said, 'I'll wait for you. Come back' (p. 265). This memory of her words haunts this passage and they re-appear in Part Three when she tells Robbie to 'come back' as he argues with Briony (p. 343). The words signify the bond between them and emphasize her faith in him despite his arrest. They also epitomize their romantic love for each other as formulated by Briony.

Part Three

This section is dominated by descriptions of Briony's training to be a nurse and continues in the third person. It explains how the period of strictures and calm is abruptly altered with the arrival of the Dunkirk wounded. There are no chapter divisions here either, which again contrasts with Part One. The narrative avoids bringing Robbie in as one of the injured men as may have been expected, and this expectation is heightened in the film adaptation when Briony mistakenly believes she has seen him outside the hospital. Instead, the dying and wounded are given their own role to condemn the violence of war and are not used to simply move the story on to a simplistic conclusion.

This is also the first time that the adult Briony is given warmer aspects to her character as she follows the orders of the formidable Sister Drummond. In McEwan's interview with John Sutherland, Sutherland touches on the deathbed scene when Briony sits with the dying Frenchman, Luc Cornet, and McEwan explains his reasons for using this: 'The central love story does not concern Briony, it concerns her sister and another man. I felt that unless I had some sort of eruption of feeling from Briony – I saw it as a love scene, even though it's a dying scene – there would be something too unreliable about her account of love' (Sutherland, 2002). He also explains why he has her stand on Westminster Bridge and note that her life is passing by in the hospital: 'I knew that by the end of this hospital section I would be jumping forward 50, 60 years, and I needed a moment of softening in Briony at the time' (Sutherland, 2002). By giving her this humanity, it becomes more likely that she at least might be attempting to atone for her sin. Without this 'softening', there is the danger she would be construed as too unbelievable and, therefore, not even ambiguous in her desire to make amends.

Part Three also contains the key rejection letter from Cyril Connolly of *Horizon*. This has already been referred to in Part Two in a letter from Cecilia to Robbie where she adds 'so at least someone can see through her wretched fantasies' (p. 212). The reply from Connolly not only signifies Briony's literary ambitions, but is also a neon light for the readers to see that this is a fiction moulded by a writer for another writer. After this is recorded, Briony sets off on her fictional quest of seeing Robbie and Cecilia to tell them she will clear his name and also witnesses the marriage of Lola and Paul Marshall.

'London, 1999'

The final section set in 1999 is partly a conclusion, as final references to Lola and Paul Marshall, Briony, Leon, Jackson and Pierrot are given, as well as indications of their lives for the past 64 years. This is also where the role of the author is examined in most detail, and where Briony is allowed to be 'pitiless' in her telling of the deaths of Cecilia and Robbie (p. 370).

The first-person narrator is used for the first time here, and it is possible to interpret this as Briony asserting her position of authority as she compares herself, as a novelist, to God. This is also where the readers are given a more personal understanding of her as she explains her recent diagnosis of vascular dementia and tells how this has to be the final draft of the novel she has been rewriting for years. The future outlook that she is given is bleak: 'Loss of memory, short- and long-term, the disappearance of single words – simple nouns might be the first to go – then language itself, along with balance, and soon after, all motor control, and finally the autonomous nervous system' (p. 355).

By giving her a direct voice, this final part delineates how this is both her last chance for finding atonement as well as introducing the most unreliable of narrators to the unwitting reading public. This short section is woven through with ambiguities as she moves between gaining the sympathy of the readers and asserting her power for the last time. It deconstructs all that has gone before and because of this it is also the most crucial of sections.

The novel is completed with her return to the Tallis home, which is now a golf course and hotel. Although it has been altered considerably, the setting is used to frame the narrative and its importance to events is signposted. The influence of the past on the present is also reiterated as some of the survivors from 1935 finally watch a performance of *The Trials of Arabella*.

Themes

The literary imagination

From the epigraph onwards, *Atonement* signals ironically the dangers of the literary imagination. As well as being an encrypted warning against being drawn into the realist narrative of Part One, it is also a playful and unsettling interpretation of how the fantasist, that is the writer, has the power to order lives.

The narrative is threaded through with literary allusions, which, depending on one's point of view, add weight to the literariness or, perhaps, bring it down with cleverness. Peter Kemp considers this element to be a distinctive bonus: 'Literary references interfuse the book. One character reads *Clarissa*, Richardson's tale of rape and attempted amends. In a college production of *Twelfth Night*, Robbie has played Malvolio, the man from below stairs whose aspirations are cruelly thwarted.' Kemp then points to the Jane Austen epigraph from *Northanger Abbey*, which he describes as the 'comedy of misplaced accusations that lead to shame' as well as the echoes of D. H. Lawrence and T. S. Eliot 'and the like', and regards all of this overt intertextuality as upholding the main theme: the 'dangers of the literary imagination' (Kemp, 2001). Finding agreement with Kemp, these repeated borrowings from and references to literature are the foundation for making this a dominant concern, and this is made apparent from the first page.

It begins with Briony introduced as the budding writer at the age of 13 as she struggles to bring her play, *The Trials of Arabella*, into production for her brother, Leon, on his return visit home. It is often repeated that alongside this ambition to be a writer is a desire for order, and this is made manifest in her attempts to take charge of both the production of the play and wider events. These two passions, for writing and order, are seen to combine with her imaginative powers as she goes on to regard Robbie as a 'maniac' after reading his sexually explicit note to Cecilia. Furthermore, Briony is also depicted and, we are to believe, depicts herself here as being caught between the two spheres of childhood and adulthood, and her reaction to reading this note demonstrates this: 'The very complexity of her feelings confirmed Briony in her view that she was entering an arena of adult emotion and dissembling from which her writing was bound to benefit' (p. 113). The temptation to use the material she has stumbled across, and to later control what happens to her advantage, is revealed to be too great to resist.

Her wish to leave fairy tales behind is evoked as an expression of her maturity, but this is confounded by her inability to see beyond the ordered binary view that is the mainstay of such fictions. This restricted perspective also helps to explain why she persists in seeing her sister as a heroine and Robbie as a villain in Part One. It is telling that after considering the letter threatened 'the order of the household' (p. 114) she is inspired to write, but can only come up with the line 'there was an old lady who swallowed a fly' (p. 115). This faltering between what she would like to write and what she is able to achieve symbolizes her childlike struggle to order her thoughts, and this is referred to again in Chapter 11 in Part One from Robbie's perspective (as filtered through the lens of Briony): 'At this stage in her life Briony inhabited an ill-defined transitional space between the nursery and adult worlds which she crossed and re-crossed unpredictably' (p. 141). Her age and her ambition mean that contrary to her externalized outrage she is as much of a threat to the order of the household as she presumes Robbie to be.

Frank Kermode's review reinforces this early version of Briony in relation to the final outcome of the novel and he emphasizes the way *Atonement* examines the role of the writer through her: 'Briony's play, *The Trials of Arabella*, written for the house party, but for various reasons not then performed, was the fantasy of a very young writer enchanted by the idea that she could in a few pages create a world complete with terrors and climaxes and a necessary sort of knowingness. The entire novel is a grown-up version of this achievement, a conflict or coalescence of truth and fantasy, a novelist's treatment of what is fantasised as fact' (Kermode, 2001). It becomes, then, a fiction that always remembers the child's ambition and tells the readers how she never relinquishes it. Her dangerous imagination, which has led to the vilification of Robbie, becomes the necessary drama of the plot. In this light, the role of the imagination is central to the writing and, consequently, places doubts over the claim that this is a work of atonement.

This doubt about Briony's authenticity, in her professed aim to atone for her sin, is made more secure on a close reading of 'London, 1999'. This may be interpreted as a first-person narrated slice of ambivalence when the novelist is described as omnipotent and the readers are jolted out of the apparently realist security of the earlier sections: 'The problem these fifty-nine years has been this: how can a novelist achieve atonement when, with her absolute power of deciding outcomes, she is also God? There is no one, no entity or higher form that she can appeal to, or be reconciled with, or that can forgive her. There is nothing outside her. In her imagination she has set the limits and the terms. No atonement for God, or novelists, even if they are atheists. It was always an impossible task, and that was precisely the point. The attempt was all' (p. 371). In this quotation, Briony simultaneously pleads for understanding while flaunting the privilege she has attached to her role.

Judith Seaboyer argues that the narrative has an ethical element in that there is this warning of the dangers of control and imagination implicit in Briony's account, but the chance that the readers may be drawn into believing this most unreliable of narrators means that it maintains an ambivalent edge: 'The process of being drawn into Briony's/McEwan's doubled narrative is a little like the process of being seduced by the attractions of Milton's Satan, and thus, as Stanley Fish has argued, experiencing in small the seduction and fall of humanity.' That is, Briony may be claiming to attempt to atone for her sin against Robbie, but she may also be accused of 'colonising' him for the sake of her writing (Seaboyer, 2005, p. 32). *Atonement* leaves these possible readings open for the readers as though to reaffirm the threat of control that has been referred to throughout.

Writing a novel

There is a crossover between the themes of the dangerous literary imagination and the art of the novel, as both are concerned with the process of writing. This is because the process of writing, and novel-writing specifically, is inscribed in the self-reflexiveness of the narrative. This is after all a novel that the readers are led to believe is written by a successful novelist (Briony) at the end of her career.

Robert MacFarlane considers the way *Atonement* 'examines its own novelistic mechanisms' as one of its greatest strengths, as it avoids the weakness of other contemporary novels when there has been only 'authorial gesturing' towards the concept of representing the past with language: 'In *Atonement*, however, McEwan focuses on the way in which we create the future by making it fit templates of the past; how the forms into which the imagination is shaped by fiction are applied to life. It is in this way, he suggests, that literature can make things happen, and not always for the good'

(MacFarlane, 2001, p. 23). To this end, McEwan's use of structuralist and poststructuralist thinking is an influence on the narrative to make this a twenty-first-century country house novel rather than a rewrite of a work by Jane Austen. This is because the possibility that language shapes us, rather than the liberal humanist belief that we control language, is made apparent in the way words have shaped the narratives of Robbie, Briony, Cecilia and McEwan. Briony and other novelists may have been endowed with greater powers, but they are still limited by the language system they are born into. Bearing this in mind, Briony's claim to be akin with God is translated as pompous as well as enervating, as her power as a writer is restricted by the available tool of language.

When interpreted as a fiction about fiction and the act of writing, the rejection letter from Cyril Connolly underscores these themes. Dominic Head regards *Atonement* as McEwan's 'most extended deliberation on the form of the novel, and the inherited tradition of modern (especially English) fiction and criticism. Austen, James, Forster, Woolf, Lawrence, Rosamund Lehmann, Elizabeth Bowen and F. R. Leavis are some of the touchstones in a treatment that is sometimes ironic, but serious in its intention.' As Head goes on to argue, the rejection letter acts as a 'locus' for the theme of the tradition of novel-writing as it foregrounds the context within which Briony begins her writing career and also gives a Connolly-inspired perspective of the twentieth-century novel (Head, 2007, pp. 156–7). As Kermode argues, this letter also introduces parody, and points to the merging between the realities of fiction and non-fiction: 'It is funny because although it sounds rather like him, Connolly would never have written such a letter; it lives, like the book as a whole, on that borderline between fantasy and fact that is indeed the territory of fiction' (Kermode, 2001).

Her rejected novella, *Two Figures by a Fountain*, is praised by

Connolly for having caught 'something unique and unexplained', but it is also criticized for owing too much to 'the techniques of Mrs Woolf' and to modernism. This novella is familiar as it is an earlier draft of her reading of Cecilia and Robbie tussling at the fountain over the vase, and the advice has been followed in this last version as Connolly advises that 'development is required' (p. 312). He also suggests that 'the backbone of a story' is needed, and asks that she creates 'some tension' (p. 314).

If distance is taken from Briony's role as creator, such advice may be expected if a more developed plot is desired, but this is also a playful ironic twist on McEwan's part as he asks the readers to have distance from the 'backbone' of the story while he reminds us again that this is a novel we are reading. Briony's creation of tension comes when she accuses Robbie of the crime he did not commit, and in terms of the chronology of the story she has already done as Connolly suggests at the age of 13. As a piece of fiction, the drama is created by the author as he or she writes, and the argument returns once more to the claim that the novelist is omnipotent. Because of this, Briony is seen to perform the role of God she has aspired to and this is a reminder of both the control of the author and the process of writing. Without the tension caused by accusing Robbie, there would be no sin to atone for and, in turn, no novel.

As tempting as it is to take Connolly's letter as a mandate on writing a novel, it is not adhered to by Briony or McEwan when the author is asked to be disengaged from war and politics: 'Since artists are politically impotent, they must use this time to develop at deeper emotional levels. Your work, your war work, is to cultivate your talent, and go in the direction it demands. Warfare, as we remarked, is the enemy of creative activity' (p. 315). As this and other works by McEwan (such as *Saturday*) testify, he refuses to

separate his art from the outside world and this has resonated in
his fiction and non-fiction throughout his career as a writer. His
concern with politics, morality and the ethical treatment of others
have been long-standing themes in his work and he has challenged
the aesthetic line of thinking that it is possible to separate art from
the society it comes out of. In *Atonement*, this is made acute in parts
Two and Three most notably, but also in the underlying conflicts of
the 1935 of Part One. Warfare is made central to the entirety of
this 'creative activity' as the main protagonists are seen to live
through fear and separation as well as being the means to deconstruct class barriers.

War

Although Part One might be described as the Jane Austen novel
McEwan had never previously written, Part Two resists any such
containment as it begins abruptly in the chaotic events sur-
rounding the Dunkirk retreat. In Part One, the sense of the
impending war is alluded to in the work of Jack Tallis and Paul
Marshall and figuratively in the rising tensions in the house, but it
is in Part Two that the narrative switches altogether to embrace
the full disparity between the then and now of peace and war.
Further to this, the urgency of the tone emphasizes the situation of
panic and this is made particularly clear in relation to the preceding section.

McEwan's desire to be faithful in this reconstruction of the
retreat and of the care taken for the injured and dying has an
ethical dimension that depends on veracity according to the detail
that still remains from this period. This perhaps explains his
extensive use of Lucilla Andrews' *No Time For Romance* in Part
Three, but this loyalty to the past also lends the narrative a
believability that is steeped in a tradition of realism and even

naturalism. The political impotency of the writer, as claimed by *Atonement*'s version of Cyril Connolly, is also made questionable as the war and its outcome (of injured and killed soldiers) is attacked for the waste that is incurred and is made graphic in the lengthy tracking shot of the Dunkirk beaches in the adaptation.

By placing the snapshot of the Dunkirk retreat after the English country house setting of Part One in the novel and film, there is an attack on not only the carnage that comes with war, but also on the hide-bound class system of middle England that is represented by the Tallis family. The descriptions of this retreat refuse to justify a blind patriotism, and also implicitly criticize the self-enclosed bourgeois that fails to see the guilt of the privileged and wealthy as represented by Paul Marshall. The theme of war encompasses wider conflicts such as class difference, as the intolerance of difference is the reason why many of the Tallises are so quick to assume Robbie is guilty of the crime he is accused of committing.

Guilt, forgiveness and atonement

Taking the lead from the title and Briony's declaration that this novel is her last attempt at atoning for her sin of lying, the related themes of guilt, atonement and forgiveness are used ambiguously as it is never made entirely certain whether she is atoning for her sins or is using the sovereignty of the author, which she aligns with God, to construct this ordered world. Because of this ambiguity, guilt and the concept of atoning are written as problematic reactions and outcomes to an immoral act. This is made more confused (and interesting) by her young age at the time she commits her crime.

Chapter 13 of Part One is significant with regard to these themes, as Briony's point of view as to why she failed to retract her statement is expanded upon here. The figurative language of the anxious bride-to-be is used when an explanation is offered for why she never told the truth after the first lie, and is also sly a reminder of her quasi-innocence: 'She was like a bride-to-be who begins to feel her sickening qualms as the day approaches, and dares not speak her mind because so many preparations have been made on her behalf' (p. 169). This apparent passivity is balanced somewhat by the claim that she also 'marched into the labyrinth of her own construction, and was too young, too awestruck, too keen to please, to insist on making her own way back' (p. 170). This swing between guilt-filled explanations and justifications reinforces the ambivalent edge to her supposed desire for atonement.

Her sense of guilt is depicted as fluctuating and this destabilizes the simplistic binaries of guilt and innocence, forgiveness and blame, and fact and fiction. For Melanie Klein, guilt is associated with love when it is interpreted as making reparations for the debt of guilt (Klein, 1937) and in *Atonement*, Briony's declared love for Cecilia and her medical prince, Robbie, drives her to unite them in fiction, and is thus seen to make partial amends for her crime. However, this is only ever partly possible as she has also been seen to create the situation she goes on to write about.

Characters

The use of shifting perspectives between many of the central characters in Part One means that the readers are given the opportunity to learn about their thoughts through the filter of Briony and this technique tallies with McEwan's professed affection for what he sees as a trait of nineteenth-century novels (Lynn, 2007). The particular use of the shifting point of view also recalls work by James and, occasionally, Woolf as he avoids being restricted by the influence of one author or movement. This becomes clearer when one analyses the different ways that characterization is developed and how characters are named.

This movement from one point of view to another lends a richness to Part One, but although perspectives are given into the various characters these are always imagined through the cipher of Briony. The fictional voice within the fictional voice is a measure of Briony's supposed control as a writer and is also a means of distancing the readers from being enveloped fully by the realism on offer.

As a novel that insists on making references to its own fictional status as well as to the process of novel writing, it is unsurprising that the construction of the characters is also hinted at. This is exemplified in Messud's explanation of how the naming of the characters reminds us of their fictionality: 'Then, too, there are the characters' names: Leon, Briony and Cecilia are overdone enough; but what of the Quincy cousins, Lola, Jackson and Pierrot? *We are characters*, these names announce. And this is a story' (Messud, 2002). Further to this, Robbie's comrades, the unlikely sounding Nettle and Mace, should also be added to this list. Messud continues by arguing that this 'frank playfulness' allows McEwan to 'follow his characters more honestly than ever before' and says this is most apparent in parts Two and Three: 'They lead us not into the psyches of the unhinged but into the psyches of ordinary people in an unhinged time' (Messud, 2002). More specifically, the characterizations of Robbie in Part Two and Briony in Part Three are determined by the way they react to the carnage he witnesses.

Briony
An understanding of the development of Briony is more difficult to negotiate or conclude when compared to other characters as she is

at various times an adolescent who wishes to take centre-stage, an unreliable narrator, an unreliable author and finally an old woman suffused with guilt for the sin she committed over 60 years ago. She is the cause of the tension that the novel depends on and is also the means for reminding the readers that this is a work of fiction. In Briony, McEwan has created a character that emphasizes that the readers do not have to have empathy with her or identify with her to enjoy the work. She is always ambiguous and is difficult to believe in, given that her lie has given the novel its drama, and so she may be regarded as a lesson in understanding ambivalence. With her crucial role in the construction of the novel, the readers are entrusted in making ethical decisions about atoning for sins without being explicitly instructed by the author (McEwan) in how to think.

The depiction of her(self) as a young girl swings between noting her innocence and guilt. Chapter 13 begins dramatically as the readers are told that, 'within the half hour Briony would commit her crime', but the guilt is undercut immediately by self-justification: 'Conscious that she was sharing the night expanse with a maniac, she kept close to the shadowed walls of the house at first, and ducked low beneath the sills whenever she passed in front of a lighted window' (p. 156).

It is repeated in Part One that she loves the thought of keeping secrets, but as an innocent child she has none to keep and her desire for order is central to her characterization at this point. It is also stated several times that her ambition to be an admired writer is necessary for an understanding of her and the lie she goes on to tell.

The news of her impending loss of memory in 'London, 1999' gives the novel yet another ironic manipulation and allows for some pathos to be added to this ambivalent construction. Her diagnosis of vascular dementia means she will soon need 'continuous care' as she will lose the ability to 'to comprehend anything at all' and she explains 'the process will be slow, but my brain, my mind, is closing down' (p. 354). Old age looks set to incapacitate her and this gives her narrative a last dramatic touch. This is because within the remit of the story the need to establish Robbie's innocence is made more urgent.

It is also through Briony that Part Three is able to document the role of the nurses in treating the wounded soldiers on their evacuation from Dunkirk and give a suggestion of how the war at this stage threatened to infiltrate lives in Britain beyond recognition: 'The Germans had reached the Channel, the British Army was in difficulties. It had all gone badly wrong in France, though no one knew on what kind of scale. This foreboding, this muted dread, was what she had sensed around her' (p. 284). The indictment of war is given a further boost after the description of Robbie's experiences, as Briony witnesses the suffering of the dying and wounded men who were also at Dunkirk. This period which is often regarded with patriotic fervour as the time of the 'Dunkirk spirit', of remaining stoic under siege, is undermined by this version of history that remembers the pain those men endured. Through Robbie and Briony, the results of war are made specific.

Robbie

Robbie is the son of Grace and Ernest Turner, and after Ernest disappeared she worked as the cleaner for the Tallises. Thanks to Jack Tallis, Robbie was supported during his time at grammar school, having won a scholarship, and after gaining a first at Cambridge he is considering studying to be a doctor (in Part One). He is working class, and the divide between him and the Tallises is broached by the education he has received. However, the differences between the two families are exposed once he is accused of harming Lola. His guilt is unquestioned as Emily, Leon and Jack prefer to accept Briony's version over his and it is possible to see him as being easy to sacrifice because of his class status.

From the beginning of Part Two, when he sees the 'unexpected detail' of a leg in a tree, the wreckage of war is unflinchingly referred to as the memories will not let him go (p. 191). This is made plain when he later thinks how the scraps of cloth he has seen nearby could have been from a child's pyjamas. This thought haunts him when he hallucinates and he thinks that he should have returned for the boy.

His thoughts are also explored as he looks back at his time in prison and reflects on how this episode has remained with him: 'Being here, sheltering in a barn, with an army in rout, where a child's limb in a tree was something that ordinary men could ignore, where a whole country, a whole civilisation was about to fall, was better than being there, on a narrow bed under a dim electric light, waiting for nothing' (p. 202). With the war, he at least has the ability to escape the blankness of prison, but his only desire is to return to England and Cecilia.

He is depicted as enduring all the misery in heroic terms in that he is an ordinary man, as Messud points out, and is caught up in extraordinary circumstances while also trying to stay alive. The narrative refuses to over-dramatize his reactions as though in respect of those who were there as, incidentally, McEwan's father was. Joe Wright, the director of the film adaptation, argues convincingly that the descriptions of Robbie's saint-like sufferance should be associated with Briony's claim of atonement, as she constructs him as the hero he was when he found the missing twins and before he was arrested (DVD, 2008). This image of him is heightened when one considers how he touches his injury in Part Two, because this has echoes of Caravaggio's painting, *Doubting Thomas*, where Thomas looks for proof of Christ's resurrection by probing his wound.

Cecilia

In Part One, Cecilia is depicted as being at an intermediary stage of her life as she has drifted through the summer without quite deciding what she wants to do next after leaving university. Chapter 2 is useful for the descriptions it gives of her state of mind earlier in the day before Robbie's arrest as it explains her restlessness: 'She could not remain here, she knew she should make plans, but she did nothing' (p. 21). It is also related that nobody is 'holding her back' and yet she resists leaving not only as a form of 'self-punishment', but also because of a desire to be needed by the family and because of half-formed thoughts of Robbie (pp. 21–22).

As with Robbie, she studied literature at Cambridge, but gained a third in comparison to his first. However, because of the regulations against women students, this was not conferred on her. Women did not receive this equal treatment at Cambridge until 1948.

She is also described in Part One as being disordered and this is made to contrast with Briony's more fastidious habits. She acts as Briony's counterpoint because she gives further emphasis to Briony's desire for order. Cecilia is also used as a counterpoint when Briony makes the decision to follow her into the controlled environment of nursing rather than university. This exemplifies Briony's self-flagellation wrapped up as atonement as well as an unspoken adherence to her sister over the rest of the family.

After the close of Part One, Briony and Robbie dominate most of the rest of the novel, with Cecilia being used at specific times as

Robbie's lover and Briony's unforgiving sister. Her letters to Robbie are a useful device for holding the narrative together as they explain what Briony has been doing for the past few years and they also remind us of the literariness of this novel. This happens ostensibly because Cecilia and Robbie draw on literary figures and use them as codes to symbolize their love in order to bypass the censor during his time in prison: 'Tristan and Isolde, the Duke Orsino and Olivia (and Malvolio too), Troilus and Criseyde, Mr Knightly and Emma, Venus and Adonis, Turner and Tallis' (p. 204).

This quotation affirms the literary status of the couple, with tongue partially in cheek, and also reminds us that this is a love story. As Briony admits in the last section, Robbie and Cecilia belong in the realm of romantic lovers and she has made them comply with the expectations that have been learned in the past. As typifies romantic love, they are separated by obstacles, such as the class system, then prison, then war, and still this does not deter them; only death can divide them before unification is possible.

The Tallises

The distance from the reader that is maintained in Part One also captures an identifiable representation of a 1930s English bourgeoisie family as they suffer from the heat on a rare hot summer's day. Although Leon says it is acceptable to break the rules on a day such as this, this idea is seen to be as insubstantial as he is always implied to be. John Mullan points out the dramatic irony behind his conversation, as Briony has already seen Robbie in the library with Cecilia, which confirmed he was the maniac she had imagined (Mullan, 2003c, p. 32). This remark by Leon also registers his lack of perception. He is able to perform to the part of acting as the social lubricant with ease, but as Cecilia argues in a letter to Robbie, he and the rest of her family are to be condemned for their belief in Robbie's guilt: 'My mother never forgave you your first. My father preferred to lose himself in his work. Leon turned out to be a grinning, spineless idiot who went along with everyone else' (p. 209). With the exception of Cecilia, the Tallis family are gradually revealed to be as dysfunctional as they are stereotypically English, and the swift movement from almost accepting Robbie as a member of the family to believing in his guilt acts as a trope for the antagonism displayed against the class outsider.

Because Part One culminates in Robbie's arrest, the section as a whole allows for a questioning of the pre-war superficial calm with the use of characters such as Leon and Emily, and also makes use of the backdrop of their opulent but crumbling home. On the surface they appear to be enviable for their privileged existences, but not far beneath they are seen to be as damaged and unoriginal as the 40-year-old house that aspires to be thought of as embodying centuries of tradition but is riddled with faults. We are told how it was acquired by the grandfather who made his money in locks and was intended to be a demonstration of his wealth. This money has also allowed the Tallises to be raised into the upper ranks of the class system, but the news that this is a privilege only recently bought means that the readers are invited to mock their position in the hierarchy that they embrace so readily.

This deconstruction of the class system through characterization is also in place in Chapter 6 of Part One when Emily lies in bed aware of the movements in the house, but is too self-absorbed and incapable to intervene in the status quo. Her migraine is the vehicle and the metaphor to explain her distance from her children, but this chapter also reveals the values associated with maintaining her position as she mentally criticizes Cecilia for wasting her time studying for a degree and hopes Leon will bring a friend home one day for her to marry, 'if three years at Girton had not made her an impossible prospect' (p. 64). Emily is drawn as pragmatic in her Englishness and mediocrity as she puts up with her husband's affairs while making claims of genteel propriety. Her relatively weak position as a married unskilled woman is tied to her being 'understanding', as the scandal caused by her sister's divorce suggests is necessary, but she is also depicted as accepting of this: 'She could send her tendrils into every room in the house, but she could not send them into the future. She also knew that, ultimately, it was her own peace of mind she strove for; self-interest and kindness were best not separated' (p. 71).

Although he is not a member of the family, Paul Marshall's visit to the house is predicated by his friendship with Leon and his membership to the right set. His success and class mean he is accepted and he is never suspected of harming Lola long after the rape takes place. Cecilia and Robbie, for example, believe Danny Hardman is the culprit. Marshall is drawn unsympathetically by an older, recalcitrant Briony and it is elemental to her atonement that she also reveals his guilt. His mismatched face is made much of and the signs of his guilt, such as the scratch on his face and the noises Emily hears upstairs, are set out with enough suggestion for him to be suspected if not initially condemned.

In 'London, 1999', he and Lola are included in the narrative most obviously because Briony has seen them. This gives her an opening to describe how they appear in old age and how they have remained untouchable and secretive since the day Lola was raped in 1935. There is something of the caricature about these villains, and the plural is used because Lola is included now by association, and this is emphasized when Lola is compared to Cruella de Vil of *The Hundred and One Dalmations* (1956) (p. 358). By describing the influence these two still have, Briony exculpates herself somewhat as well, and gives the narrative closure as she ties up the loose ends of what happened to some of the key characters.

The cousins from the north

Lola, Jackson and Pierrot are introduced as the 'cousins from the north' in Chapter 1 of Part One, as Briony considers the production of her play. They are immediately cast as outsiders and antagonistic to her love of order, because their arrival at the house has threatened to disrupt proceedings (p. 8). This is later seen to occur more vigorously when the twins go missing and Lola is raped, but before these events the twins are described as at first reluctant to perform in the play and Lola is characterized as being even more precocious than Briony. They are the catalysts for the main action that leads to Robbie's arrest and are barely realized beyond Briony's child-like perception of them.

They are also the children of divorcing parents and their embarrassment with this situation is a means to re-enact the stigma associated with family breakdown in this period. This stigma is also the implied reason why Jack and Emily are still married even though their relationship is no longer fulfilling or happy.

The servants

Atonement is concerned primarily with the Tallis family and Robbie, rather than the servants, and so it is understandable that these play only minor roles. The most notable one is Grace, as she is Robbie's mother, and her inclusion adds to the development of his characterization. Her position as cleaner is a sign of her social status and signifies the gulf between Robbie's and Cecilia's parents. She was given patronage by Jack Tallis after her husband deserted her, and Robbie has also benefited from this in that he received a university education that would have otherwise been impossible given the period and his class. When the Tallises are quick to believe in Robbie's guilt, however, it is possible to see that this was always a kindness that could be revoked and the acceptance of Grace and her son is seen to have been based on whim rather than loyalty.

Danny Hardman is another minor character, but is of interest because he adds some mystery to the events of Part One. Earlier in the day, Robbie notices him leering at Lola and he is used as a red herring to distract Robbie and Cecilia, if not the readers, from the truth. Like Robbie, he also becomes a scapegoat for the actions of Paul Marshall. In Briony's fictional account of her meeting with Robbie and Cecilia in Part Three, she explains that Danny was not guilty of the crime as they had supposed. Their belief that he had been the culprit (rather than Marshall) suggests once more that the hierarchical class system allows those in the higher reaches to be seen as blameless despite the evidence.

Metaphors and symbolic language

The vase

The vase, which Cecilia and Robbie struggle over at the fountain, is elemental to the plot, as Briony's imaginative misunderstanding of this scene feeds into her castigation of him later. Its importance is later indicated in the way she uses this scene in the story she sends to Connolly.

It serves the symbolic purpose of signposting the family's pretensions, yet its journey to the Tallis home is almost as convoluted as the return of the heirloom watch that belongs to Butch in *Pulp Fiction* (1994). It is a gift from when Uncle Clem served in the First

World War and is valued for this rather than its heritage; it also acts as a connection between Robbie and Cecilia.

The damage it undergoes is also of further relevance to the novel. Kermode notes the triangular pieces that break off into the fountain and says in an aside how 'triangles form a leitmotif for readers to puzzle over', and also explains that the breakage resonates later: 'The wounded vase will later meet an even worse fate, and this premonitory damage echoes what happens to other fragile objects highly valued but easily ruined, such as Cecilia's virginity, and indeed life itself' (Kermode, 2001). Emily informs Briony in a letter in Part Three of its final outcome: 'Wretched Betty dropped Uncle Clem's vase carrying it down and it shattered on the steps. She said the pieces had simply come away in her hand, but that was hardly to be believed' (p. 279). In its last fall, the vase becomes a metaphor for the tenuous hold we have on objects and each other. In addition, Emily's disbelief at Betty's explanation is in keeping with her disregard for the lower orders that she has demonstrated on other occasions.

The Tallis house

Despite initially appearing to exude grandeur and upper-class status, the Tallis house is revealed to be less than both these claims: 'Morning sunlight, or any light, could not conceal the ugliness of the Tallis home – barely forty years old, bright orange brick, squat, lead-paned baronial Gothic, to be condemned one day in an article by Pevsner, or one of his team, as a tragedy of wasted chances, and by a younger writer of the modern school as "charmless to a fault"' (p. 19).

Metaphorically, it represents the family's push for respectability in that it was bought by Cecilia's grandfather who made his fortune 'with a series of patents on padlocks, bolts, latches and hasps', having grown up over an ironmonger's shop (p. 19). With this new money, he bought the family the shell of status that his descendents have taken for granted, but its faults reflect the sham of the class-ridden society. That is, the house appears to be of a superior quality, but when one looks more closely it becomes apparent that it does not deserve the merit it expects. Through this representation of the house, then, it is possible to see a figurative criticism of class bias.

Because it was paid for with the money grandfather made on locks and bolts, it also represents the centrality of secrecy to this novel.[1] *Atonement* begins with an explanation of Briony's 'passion for secrets' and, although at this point she does not have any, she goes on to keep the falsity of her accusation quiet (p. 5). Similarly, Lola also never mentions the truth about the identity of her attacker, and her marriage to Paul Marshall tells us she never will.

The house is returned to in 'London, 1999' and is now known as Tilney's Hotel. Its rebranding signifies the post-war change in times for the Tallis family while also indicating how the wider society has become more leisure-fixated. The name Tilney is also a reference back to the epigraph, as the Tilney family appear in *Northanger Abbey*.

Water

The use of water as a motif in the film version of *Atonement* is discussed more fully in 'Performance and Adaptation', but it is also relevant to analyse its usage in the novel here. The artificial lake and fountain add to the image of surface upper middle-class status. Again, it is only the appearance of belonging that is signposted, because the lake is artificial and the fountain has the half-scale

---

[1] Thanks must go to Dr Ana Maria Sanchez-Arce for this insight.

reproduction of Bernini's *Triton*. To add to this emphasis on fakery, the Triton is described as such: 'The muscular figure, squatting so comfortably on his shell, could blow through his conch a jet only two inches high, the pressure was so feeble, and water fell back over his head, down his stone locks and along the groove of his powerful spine, leaving a glistening dark green stain' (p. 18). Both the lake and fountain represent the ambition of the family, though, even if the desired effect is not achieved. It is telling that when Briony visits her former home for the last time for her birthday treat, the lake has disappeared along with the island temple and the island is necessarily no longer an island. The land is now used as a golf course and the lake is not needed, and metaphorically it is seen to be as redundant as the class aspirations of the Tallis family.

Water also symbolizes union, as it is at the fountain where Cecilia and Robbie are first seen to come together, and safety. This latter point is made in Part Two when Robbie forces himself to reach the sea despite his injury.

The Army Amo bar

Paul Marshall is set to make a fortune with this new chocolate bar when, as he hopes, a war will come about if 'Mr Hitler did not pipe down' (p. 50). Bearing in mind this is said in 1935, the bar represents how for some the possibility of profiting from war is of more interest than brokering for peace or challenging fascism on moral grounds. Because of this, Marshall's lack of scruples are reflected in his desire for its success, and his boasts to Cecilia and Robbie enhance his anti-hero status: '... there was even a chance that the bar could be part of the standard-issue ration pack; in that case, if there were to be a general conscription, a further five factories would be needed ...' (p. 50).

He also uses the bar as a means to talk to the children and when it is discovered that he is the one who goes on to rape Lola, the Army Amo may be interpreted as a poisoned chalice. As with its creator, it appears to be innocent but it is not and never has been.

Narrative devices

Point of view

As stated previously, the use of the shifting point of view in Part One allows the third-person narrator to give the perspectives of various characters as the day unfolds. This device allows for a distance to be maintained as Briony purports to interpret the opinions of others in her version of her atonement. This has the intended effect of giving the readers glimpses into the consciousness and emotions of characters and is, then, a useful means for the development of characterization.

Unreliable narrator

The unreliable narrator is a literary device that has been employed in works such as *The Turn of the Screw* (1898) by Henry James and *Wuthering Heights* (1847) by Emily Brontë. This is when a first-person narrator is used and the subjective responses and interpretations of this character are revealed. This means that the narration is permeated with ambiguity, as, again, the narrator is deemed unreliable.

The unreliable narrator is used in 'London, 1999' as the novel shifts finally to Briony's first-person account. It is possible to see that the device is being used playfully, because Briony's earlier lie about Robbie and her explanation of how the novelist is comparable to God already mean that she is clearly difficult to trust. This exaggerates the subjectivity of her narration, which is always going to be biased anyway as it is in the first person, and means that the titular claim of 'atonement' should be interpreted with caution.

Letters

Letters are used as a means to uphold the authentic strain of both parts Two and Three, as Briony coaxes the readers into believing this is the truth that is being laid out. They are also useful for explaining the perspectives of characters such as Cecilia. Rather than simply recounting the past, this format gives the views of the writer as is true to the spirit of the novel (especially Part One) where the narrative switches between the perspectives of the main characters. These letters allow for a first-person insight into the thoughts of a character and thereby give another aspect of their consciousness.

These letters also act as a further textual layer embedded in a narrative that is already self-conscious about using words to give order to the past. It is telling that it is a letter from Robbie to Cecilia – which refers to her 'cunt' – that initially condemns Robbie from Briony's immature point of view. Because it is the wrong letter, and the worst of Freudian slips, his arrest that evening is made all the more poignant.

Briony's faith in the written word may be seen to also extend to her old age as she depends on letters for documentary evidence in the shaping of her narrative. This is made definite in 'London, 1999' when she refers to the assistance she has had from old Mr Nettle and the Imperial War Museum. Furthermore, the letter from Connolly is included as another supposed touch of realism.

The revelation

Briony's late revelation that she is the author, and that Robbie died at Dunkirk and Cecilia was killed at Balham station are examined by Mullan in 'Beyond Fiction' and described as an aspect of the metanarrative (a narrative about the narrative). In this article, he also clarifies the distinction between metafiction and metanarrative to explain more fully how McEwan has drawn the reader into a complex web of self-reflexivity: 'Metafiction is persistently self-referential, like Italo Calvino's *If on a Winter's Night a Traveller*, which, from its first sentence, makes a story of how reader and writer conspire to make a story. McEwan's metanarrative, however, is a revelation withheld. Some readers have felt cheated by it, like viewers of *Dallas* who were suddenly shown by desperate script-writers that the traumatic events of many previous episodes were just Pam Ewing's "dream".' He also describes the metanarrative as the short final section 'that accounts for its existence' (Mullan, 2003d, p. 32). The disappointment that doubtless accompanies the news that we are asked to believe this has been Briony's creation all along may be contrasted with how this alters the interpretation of the novel for the better as yet another layer of meaning has been added.

The use of a metanarrative and metafiction need not be seen as mutually exclusive as Mullan implies, though. *Atonement* is not overly literal in the way it demonstrates that this is a fiction about fiction, but its repeated allusions to the novel-writing process and to the dangers of the literary imagination, let alone the many self-conscious literary references, mean that from the epigraph onwards this novel hints to the readers this is a novel. It is perhaps down to the skill of the writer that this is done implicitly enough for the first-time reader to feel as cheated by the metanarrative as *Dallas* fans were by Pam Ewing's dream.

In his interview with David Lynn, McEwan explains the readers were let off lightly with the 'tricksey' elements, as he wrote but discarded an 'About the Author' section that was devoted to Briony. This told of how he imagined her career, which 'dipped for a while, but then in the sixties she was taken up by Virago press and her novel *The Ducking Stool* was made into a film with Julie Christie'. He was also going to have her death as July 2001 when he finished writing it, but thought he should set the readers 'down on *terra firma*' instead (Lynn, 2007).

The moral dilemma of fictionalizing the truth

As a historical novel that uses the Second World War as a context, *Atonement* has a relationship with the past that, simply put, means it fictionalizes events that have occurred. His use of research in the Imperial War Museum, of the stories his father told him and Lucilla Andrews' account have been referred to by him as narratives that enabled him to come as close as he could to retrieving the past.

His response to the charge of plagiarism, which is one most writers would dread, came in the form of an explanation of how he was partly inspired by his father's stories of his time spent in the war, which included being in the Dunkirk retreat. In 'An Inspiration, Yes. Did I Copy from Another Author? No', he outlines how his father's experience of reaching the beaches to be evacuated and his later stay in hospital were used in parts Two and Three: 'When I came to write *Atonement*, my father's stories, with automatic ease, dictated the structure; after I finished the opening section, set in 1935, Dunkirk would have to be followed by the reconstruction of a 1940 hospital.' He cites the specific instance of when his father was shot in the legs and then 'teamed up' with another man who had been injured in the arms, and between them they managed to ride a motorcycle to reach the Dunkirk beaches and finally safety (McEwan, 2006b). This account is used in Part Two and helps to accentuate the desperate need for the allied soldiers to reach the beaches in time.

He acknowledges his debt to Lucilla Andrews' autobiography, *No Time for Romance*, here and elsewhere (including in the Acknowledgements page in *Atonement*) for the rich detail it gave him of the nurses' training and of how the arrival of the Dunkirk wounded was coped with. He describes this as a 'shared reality' and, therefore, makes it explicit that he regards such contemporary accounts as being in the public realm. In this article, he also stresses his desire to be authentic and to act in good faith in his account of the war: 'In writing about wartime especially, it seems like a form of respect for the suffering of a generation wrenched from their ordinary lives to be conscripted into a nightmare' (McEwan, 2006b).

It is ironic, of course, that the author of a novel such as *Atonement*, which deconstructs the privileged status of the author while also reinforcing it, should ask to be believed about his writing practices. It is also relevant to remember that the 'shared reality' he draws upon is embroidered with his fictionalized version along with stories he has heard in his childhood. Just like Briony, the author has the power to order the narrative just as he or she chooses.

Tim Gauthier explains the unsolvable difficulties for the contemporary writer that engages with history: 'Like Byatt and a number of other contemporary writers, McEwan exhibits a paradoxical relationship with the past. He knows that it cannot be known, but this does not prevent him from trying to know it. And the truths that are unearthed, whether they be the *real* truths of the past or not, are not any less for that' (Gauthier, 2006, p. 23). Gauthier uses *Black Dogs* as the means to make this point, but it also stands for later works such as *Atonement* as the past is evoked with recognition of the influence of postmodernism as well as demonstrating an abiding desire for truth.

Ideas associated with postmodernism expose the difficulty, if not impossibility, of knowing the absolute truth, and this is because postmodern thinking has destabilized the concept of defining absolute meanings. It is a given that *Atonement* draws on historical truths, or as close as McEwan is able to manage this, but because he also draws on the influence of postmodernism in 'London, 1999' he asks the readers to adopt a position that both accepts and refuses the absolute. Using a framework of Gayatori Spivak's for the purpose of this reading, it is possible to argue that the novel offers a strategic essentialist understanding of truth and demonstrates the ethical need to find it even if it is no longer an absolute post-poststructuralist theory. This is a refashioning of Spivak's theory as it was originally used in the context of querying the possibility of speaking as a subaltern, but is useful in this instance for understanding how *Atonement* queries the division between fact and fiction while also representing the devastation caused by a lie. As seen in the first chapter, 'Novelist', McEwan subscribes to the need for truth and questions the relativism of postmodernism. It is also evident in *Atonement* that the relativity of truth and lies is exposed via the use of Briony and her ambiguous hold on her version of reality which is laid out as truth. By using a strategically essentialist position in order to broach the subject of ethical responsibility in a culture where absolute truth is diminished, McEwan manages to show that it is still worth searching for and adhering to. Put more lucidly, despite the boundary between fact and fiction becoming blurred as postmodern thinking questions the concept of one reality and one truth, McEwan uses Briony's lie and her ambivalent relationship to versions of truth to demonstrate the necessity of ethics.

Conclusion

As Head argues, however, the ambiguous construction of Briony and the reiteration of the themes of guilt and atonement mean that the ethical and moral position of the novel may also be viewed as murky: 'The circularity of this guilt-atonement reveals a general observation about the equivocation of novel-writing, shown to be in an uneasy and shifting relationship to any construction of morality' (Head, 2008, p. 174). This uneasiness filters through, as the readers become unsettled by Briony's supposed final truth, and with the greater understanding passed down from Plato that the poets are liars.

The popular and critical success of *Atonement* has depended on this ability to draw its readers in by telling them a story while at the same time constantly reminding us that this is a fiction. The development of character through the use of shifting point of view, the organization of the structure and the multiple levels of meaning that are broached in the themes all affirm McEwan's technical skill.

3

Critical Reception

Reviews of *Atonement* in the broadsheets and literary journals were, with the odd exception, positive bordering on congratulatory. At this point in his career, McEwan was a mainstay of British fiction and had come to be regarded as a respected author and one of the key writers of his generation. With this novel, he impressed the fans and non-committed alike and it was quickly spotted as his most compelling work to date. Robert MacFarlane's review for *The Times Literary Supplement*, for example, considers it to be his 'finest achievement', as the dust jacket proclaims, and supplements this by saying that although the publishers will always try to sell their products, 'in this case they are triumphantly right' (MacFarlane, 2001, p. 23).

Despite the plaudits, McEwan continues to be cautious in his expectations of the critics and it appears that this in turn influences his writing. When asked by David Lynn if he ever thinks about the audience he is writing for, McEwan responded that rather than having a reader in mind he has a 'kind of being' which he imagines as his most undermining of reviewers: 'I have a kind of being, not really a reader, a kind of entity whose dominant disposition is utter scepticism. And this being wears a constant snarl, and is always muttering "come off it, you're never going to get away with that", or "this is feeble". It's all the hostile reviews or reviewers that I've ever had in my life. And it's quite a useful being' (Lynn, 2007). A perspective such as this shows not only his guarded opinion of the critics, but also a welcome modesty considering his international reputation.

The flattering comments with regard to *Atonement* were not restricted just to British-based reviews. Tom Shone in *The New York Times* describes it as McEwan's 'most complete and compassionate work to date' (Shone, 2002) and Claire Messud goes further and begins her review by comparing the reading of his prose to meeting 'an extremely good-looking person', as there is a 'confusion of expectations'. She goes on to explain that 'good looks betoken nothing certain about their possessor', but *Atonement* meets the expectations roused and she concludes with this elaborate praise: 'We see at last that the beauty of the conjuring is indeed enough; and that its meaning – in all its ambiguities – lies before us' (Messud, 2002).

Such enthusiasm, even effusiveness may seem to be too uncritical and too willing to fall in love with the English setting perhaps, or with the surprise that Briony has directed the narrative from the beginning. A closer examination of the book's reception demonstrates that it is the technical expertise that tends to beguile the critics the most. Frank Kermode compares the writing to that of Henry James, and not just because of the similarities with *What Maisie Knew*: 'Ian McEwan's new novel, which strikes me as easily his finest, has a frame that is properly hinged and jointed and apt for the conduct of the "*march of action*", which James described as "the only thing that really, for *me* at least, will *produire* L'OEUVRE". Not quite how McEwan would put it, perhaps, but still the substance of his method, especially if one adds a keen technical interest in another Jamesian obsession, the point of view' (Kermode, 2001). The comparison with James's technical skill is given weight by the analysis that Kermode offers. He explains his interpretation with reference to the 'march of action' and point of view and with regard to *Atonement* the interest in the latter is most marked in the use of shifting perspectives in Part One.

Just as Kermode draws parallels between McEwan and Henry James, Geoff Dyer in the *Guardian* argues that there is parity between McEwan, Virginia Woolf and D. H. Lawrence, as each one has demonstrated the 'transformation' of individuals. By placing McEwan in such company both critics make a tacit request to have him placed in the modern canon of authors. According to Dyer, Woolf and Lawrence have helped to bring this transformation about and McEwan has developed this: 'McEwan uses his novel to show how this subjective or interior transformation can now be seen to have interacted with the larger march of twentieth-century history' (Dyer, 2001). The appeal of *Atonement* for Dyer rests in its breadth rather than in what may be seen as its gimmicks (such as Briony's final revelation), and the main interest lies in its understanding of literature and in the way this is tied to the historical process of change. By echoing the voices of other writers and making their work new in his revitalized use of realism and modernism, McEwan is seen to have the capacity his prodigy Briony has always hoped for. This reading by Dyer should not be underestimated as, although it attempts implicitly to predict the future of the value of *Atonement* in ranking McEwan alongside such accepted literary figures, and therefore runs the risk of being seen as prematurely confident, this contemporary response is one that has been echoed by many.

The emotional resonance of the narrative attracts Peter Kemp in *The Sunday Times* and he applauds it for the various levels it works on: 'Subtle as well as powerful, adeptly encompassing comedy as well as atrocity, *Atonement* is a richly intricate book. Unshowy symmetries and patterns underlie its emotional force and psychological compulsion.' He also points to the effectiveness of the theme of the dangers of the literary imagination, as many critics have, and argues this is returned to persistently: 'The instinct for order (so important in the army, Robbie finds; so beneficial in the hospital, Briony discovers) proves of more ambiguous effect when the artistic temperament impinges on life's confusions' (Kemp, 2001, p. 46). As Kemp points out, the desire for order is seen to be threatened or undone by Briony, who personifies this dangerous literary imagination. It is also deeply ironic that the urge to control events is connected to the way the action spirals out of her reach.

Given the overwhelming praise of the majority of responses, Anita Brookner's review for *The Spectator* is illuminating because it is one of the few negative ones. Her main criticism is that she regards it as being unconvincing, but she also resents the change in form and content when compared to his earlier works: 'McEwan's novels are normally thrilling examinations of various nasty situations. Here his suave attempts to establish morbid feelings as inspiration for a life's work – and for that work to be crowned with success – are unconvincing. *Atonement* is in itself a morbid procedure. If it were more palliative penance could be embraced with total confidence' (Brookner, 2001). In relation to this point that it is 'unconvincing', Brookner is also troubled by what she sees as gaps in authenticity in that we are expected to believe in too many improbable things, such as the Meissen vase being immersed in a fountain that has a copy of Bernini's *Triton*, and in the night being too dark for Lola's attacker to be seen. This line of argument that 'authenticity is indeed a problem here' is based on the perceived need for believability, which one could argue is not necessarily a prerequisite of so-called good fiction. In contrast with Brookner's interpretation, MacFarlane raptures over the early slow pace and the way the narrative sets the scene: 'Nobody comes, nobody goes. McEwan continues to describe, with characteristic limpidity, the house and the dynamics of its inhabitants. His patience is doubly effective, for it generates not only an authentic environment in which the tragedy can eventually unfurl, but also has an ever-burgeoning sense of menace' (MacFarlane, 2001, p. 23).

The questioning of the believability is also balanced by Kermode's point that this is (after all) a work of fiction. He also reasons that this is a self-consciously fictional work and that the letter purporting to be from Cyril Connolly, for example, is a parody of his writing and is, like the novel, 'on that borderline between fantasy and fact that is indeed the territory of fiction' (Kermode, 2001). This reference reiterates the way McEwan uses the narrative to draw the readers into a realist landscape as he also reminds them that it is a novel that they are reading.

Brookner raises her personal concerns with *Atonement*, as well as pointing out that Briony seeks reparation rather than atonement, but she seems to have overlooked the use of Briony as the novelist and how we are led to believe that this is her version of events. Brookner also interprets the ending as being 'too lenient' to Briony as she is now 'elderly and celebrated' and should have told the truth back in 1935. The unreliability of Briony as a witness has been established on the night she falsely accuses Robbie, and as the novelist she is in the position to shape the perspectives of the characters as she chooses. If these aspects are not evaluated, then the irony of Briony manipulating the readers as well as her family is also missed. It is as though Brookner has forgotten this joke on the readers, which in turn suggests that when Briony compares herself favourably to God in 'London, 1999' this is taken only at face value.

Whereas Brookner is critical of the moral ambivalence exhibited by Briony, Kemp interprets this as a central element of the novel: 'Whatever equivocations linger around Briony's behaviour, though, there's no doubt about McEwan's superb achievement in this book, which combines a magnificent display of the powers of imagination with a probing exploration of them' (Kemp, 2001, p. 46). Kermode is similarly praising of the edge that is maintained by the ambivalence displayed through Briony. Critics generally subscribe to the fair play rule of reviewers not revealing the end of the novel under examination and, as he admits, this limits the overview they are able to give the readers. He goes on to point out, nevertheless, that despite the title Briony does not achieve the proposed aim and is grateful for this: 'The title of the book seems to suggest that Briony will do something by way of atonement, but nothing quite fitting that description seems to occur' (Kermode, 2001).

Conclusively, *Atonement* received the amount of attention one would expect from a work by or associated with McEwan, but the commendations for the book in particular returned consistently to the claim that this is his most impressive work to date. The merit is based on the technical skill of holding the separate sections together, as well as the demonstrable literary quality that is apparent in the comparisons with writers such as James and Woolf.

· **4**

Novel's Performance and Adaptation

In terms of sales, *Atonement* is a national and international bestseller and has been translated into a number of languages including Spanish, Dutch and Portuguese. Its sales were increased due to the tie-in publication with the release of the film version and it has been the recipient of a number of awards. These include the WH Smith Literary Prize, the National Book Critics' Circle Award, the Santiago Prize for the European Novel and the *Los Angeles Times* Prize for Fiction.

McEwan already has a connection with the film industry, having written screenplays, and some of his works have also been adapted for film prior to *Atonement* (2007). These include *The Comfort of Strangers* (1990), *The Cement Garden* (1993) and *Enduring Love* (2004). As a measure of his kudos, the screenplay for the latter was written by Harold Pinter. It is perhaps in keeping with the popularity of the novel that *Atonement* the film has so far been the most high-profile of his works to be adapted.

The Working Title Films adaptation of *Atonement* premiered at the Venice Film Festival in September 2007 as part of an extensive publicity drive. The reception from the critics may have been mixed, but for a time it was the great British film of the year as it was nominated for seven Academy Awards in 2008 and won a Golden Globe and a BAFTA for Best Film. Reviews varied from claiming it is 'masterly', by Philip French in the *Observer*, to proposing it demonstrates how 'pointless' adaptations can be (A. O. Scott, 2007).

In his review of the novel, Tom Shone sees the opening as having the potential of being a Merchant Ivory production in the future with its setting of the English country house and the centrality of the Tallis family (Shone, 2002). As he goes on to concede, this would never be possible given the material, but the film version of *Atonement* (2007), directed by Joe Wright and adapted by Christopher Hampton, capitalizes on its depiction of an upper middle-class English family in the 1930s in these early pre-war scenes. The elderly Briony is played by Vanessa Redgrave and her inclusion, along with Keira Knightley and James McAvoy, invites us to see this as a British star vehicle for the international market.

The reception of the film

In comparison with the favourable book reviews, the adaptation to film in 2007 had a more lukewarm reception. James Christopher for *The Times* points out it was one of the 'great hopes' for British cinema for that year, but thinks it fails to merit the attention it has been given, particularly when the action moves from 1935 to the Second World War: 'The moment Robbie is jailed, the credibility of Wright's film starts coming apart. The story takes a rude melodramatic knapsack off to war, and an older Briony (played by

Romola Garai) signs up as a nurse and tries to atone for her ghastly sin' (Christopher, 2007).

A similar criticism is made in *The New York Times* by Scott who also regards it as becoming weaker as it moves away from the first scenes of 1935. Scott argues that it is not that this is a 'bad literary adaptation', but that it is instead 'an almost classic example of how pointless, how diminishing, the transmutation of literature into film can be. The respect that Mr Wright and Mr Hampton show to Mr McEwan is no doubt gratifying to him, but is fatal to their own project' (Scott, 2007). This loyalty to the novel has also meant that the abrupt shift to the war has not translated to the screen as would have been hoped. Visually, the separate sections have the effect of making the film disjointed, and if a smoother movement through time is required, the adaptation needs to steer away from the novel more obviously.

Cosmo Landesman offers another negative perspective and suggests this is a film that has nothing new to offer: 'Irritatingly, *Atonement* gives us the worst of two worlds stylistically: it exploits the taste and nostalgia for 1930s and 1940s Hollywood melodrama, yet it has an annoying postmodern knowingness to it. At its heart is a concern with the unreliability of narrative, be it that of a 13-year-old girl one hot summer's day or that of British history. Thus, when Robbie, who chooses the army instead of prison, winds up at Dunkirk, waiting for evacuation, we see that episode in a different light. Instead of a heroic exodus, we get a nightmarish vision of horses being shot and men going crazy' (Landesman, 2007). Both the book and film elaborate on a version of the retreat that goes against the traditional view that it was as Landesman claims 'a heroic exodus', which has been the prevailing British ideology since the Second World War. Robbie is constructed as a hero, but no comfort in defeat is offered for the viewers or readers, as this episode is captured as bloody and ultimately wasteful. By representing this significantly precarious moment in British history in such a way – that is, not patriotically – McEwan and Wright will be open for criticism (and especially from those who see such depictions as disloyal). When the film is seen as a critique of destruction, however, it is not so easy to condemn.

For a more positive account of the film, French in the *Observer* considers the later sequences of the 1935 section as being handled with 'immense narrative verve' and praises the process of adaptation overall despite the occasional melodramatic touches: 'What the film brings to the book, apart from excellent performances, are fine images and a powerful period atmosphere' (French, 2007, p. 18). It is also of note that whereas Scott and Landesman question the use of the long tracking shot of the beaches at Dunkirk, French regards this as one of the finest aspects of the film: 'There is a virtuoso long take, lasting five to six minutes, that belongs beside long takes by Hitchcock, Welles, Jancso, Antonioni, and Angelopoulos' (French, 2007, p. 18). By promoting this particular shot, French makes the case for the artistic remit as well as defending this deconstruction of the Dunkirk spirit.

Analysis

Negative criticisms levelled at the adaptation include the accusation by Scott that it follows the novel too closely, yet superficially, and describes it as being 'piously rendered' by Hampton (Scott, 2007). His main dispute with the film comes at the expense of a comparison with the novel: 'Mr McEwan's prose pulls you in immediately and drags you through an intricate, unsettling story, releasing you in a shaken wrung-out state. The film, after a tantalizing start, sputters to a halt in a welter of grandiose imagery and hurtling montage' (Scott, 2007). An interpretation such as this is in opposition to Brian McFarlane's *Novel to Film* (1996), which explains how 'fidelity criticism' has tended to favour novels over films as it 'depends on a notion of the text as having and rendering up to the (intelligent) reader a single, correct "meaning" which the filmmaker has either adhered to or in some sense violated or tampered with' (McFarlane, 1996, p. 8). By questioning the primacy of the novel, McFarlane enables an analysis of the adaptation in its own right: 'The stress on fidelity to the original undervalues other aspects of the film's intertextuality. By this, I mean those non-literary, non-novelistic influences at work on any film, whether or not it is based on a novel' (McFarlane, 1996, p. 21). He follows this up by explaining that the novel is just one element of the film's intertextuality and aspects such as the actors used, the 'cultural climate', the director's influence and the 'prevailing parameters of cinematic practice' should also be brought into the evaluation (McFarlane, 1996, p. 22). Although he refutes a straightforward hierarchy of a novel being preferred over the film, he also adds that the adaptation does not stand alone either and comparisons are inevitable if the book has been read before viewing the film.

As a film that is concerned with the way a writer manipulates narratives, it should be said that it is difficult to separate the connectedness between this particular novel and film, even when one takes McFarlane's point into account about showing fair recognition to adaptations. The opening credits and first scene inform the viewers immediately of the role the writer takes in this work, as a tap of keys from a typewriter spells out the title and the opening scene of summer 1935. When the camera then shifts from the nursery toys to focus on Briony typing her final version of *The*

Trials of Arabella, her youthful yet earnest ambition to be a writer is imprinted on the screen. French interprets this opening as a wider metaphor for the film and the novel: '*Atonement* begins with the film's title and its setting (the summer of 1935) loudly printed out by a manual typewriter, thus implanting in our minds that what we are about to experience is a literary work and indeed it is about fiction itself, its purpose and its morality' (French, 2007, p. 18).

The main score, which is composed by Dario Marienelli (and who is the recipient of the only Academy Award for the film), also includes the thread of the sound of typing to add urgency. This occurs, for example, when Briony is searching for her mother to show her this new venture as a playwright. In an otherwise condemnatory review, Scott interprets these early scenes in the country house as relatively praiseworthy and makes reference to the unifying effect of the typist at work: 'This charged, hardly unfamiliar atmosphere provides, in the first section of the film, some decent, suspenseful fun, a rush of incident and implication. Boxy cars rolling up the drive; whispers of scandal and family secrets; coitus interruptus in the library, all set to the implacable rhythm of typewriter keys' (Scott, 2007). Because Robbie is also shown sat typing his letter to Cecilia, in which he refers to her 'cunt' and which Briony goes on to see as proof that he is a sex maniac on Lola's prompting, the connection and difference between Briony and Robbie is made graphic. Both have been captured as authors, but it is Briony who takes and keeps control of the plot.

As with the novel, her influence on the arrangements of events in the 1935 section is explained with subtlety as it maintains a similar shift between points of view, and this is done through the replaying of key scenes. This is given most attention when Briony looks through the window and sees Robbie and Cecilia at the fountain. Her shock, which is based on misinterpretation, is explained by the replay where the viewers hear the dialogue between Robbie and Cecilia which Briony has been excluded from. The clue remains that this is her story, though, as her appearance at the window frames both versions of this narrative of the two figures by the fountain.

The centrality of Briony and the theme of her dangerous literary imagination are both maintained in the film and, as mentioned in the bonus scenes, this is brought about visually by giving the three different actors who play her at 13, as a young woman, and at the age of 77, the same hairstyle of a bob and a noticeable facial birthmark. Because it is unlikely that Briony's hair has stayed the same for over 60 years, this also has the effect of emphasizing that this is a fiction that she, McEwan and Wright have created. As with the novel, her final revelation acts as a conclusion and is allowed to have the same unsettling impact as it undoes the reality that we have already seen, of Robbie and Cecilia reunited in her flat. The use of the visual medium is made relevant as Briony gives away the secret that this is her refashioning of the story in an interview for television with Anthony Minghella playing the part of interviewer.

As well as holding the narrative together with Briony and the theme of writing, immersion in water is another recurring motif and this is used to create a chain of signifiers that signal figurative rebirths and the death of Cecilia. When Cecilia plunges into the fountain to retrieve the broken pieces of the vase, and to demonstrate her recently learned maturity to Robbie, and when Robbie is viewed bathing and Cecilia drowns after the explosion at the underground station, the film uses this element as an equalizer and as a trope to deconstruct the apparently stable hierarchies of class difference. Water washes away the sins, perhaps, but it is also used to form a connection between the lovers. This is used most effectively with the cut from Cecilia diving into the lake to Robbie sitting up in the bath after being immersed.

It is also the means for heightening Robbie's hallucinatory state at Dunkirk, as well as emphasizing his and his mother's virtue. This comes when he imagines his mother has taken off his boots and then washes his feet. The image of the mother showing love for her son is overlaid with the idea that she and Robbie are above reproach as the washing of feet also alludes to Jesus' selfless service.

Peter Childs regards the use of 'water, mirrors, and the transparency of barriers' as a 'series of identity motifs' and also demonstrates this with reference to the cut from Cecilia diving to Robbie surfacing from the bath water (Childs, 2008, p. 151). As stated, he points out that windows act as transparent barriers, and this is made particularly significant when Briony watches Robbie being taken away after being arrested. This barrier is also in place when she watches him and Cecilia at the fountain.

One of the key features of the film is the long tracking shot of the recreated chaos on the beach at Dunkirk as the Allies attempt to make their escape. The uneven reception given to the film on its release may be measured by critics' views of this scene. Whereas French regards this as evidence of 'masterly' cinematography, others have been lukewarm at most in their appraisals. It lasts for just over five minutes as the panorama includes fear and violence and a moving Ferris wheel, and it is as though the film stands still in time to encompass this landscape where horses are shot and Bibles are burned so they will not fall into enemy hands.

Peter Bradshaw wonders in his review if this film will not be populist enough to be as successful as he thinks it deserves to be: 'There are moments – delirious, languorous, romantic moments – when this film appears to have the lineaments of a classic. Yet could it be that its epic, haunting story of tragic love in the Second World War is too oblique and opaque, with too complex an enigma at its heart, to press the right commercial buttons?' (Bradshaw, 2007, p. 9). As Bradshaw suggests, whether it receives high box-office sales or not, the quality of the adaptation will ensure it a longevity of its own apart from its connection with the well-sold novel.

· **5**

Further Reading and
Discussion Questions

Introduction

As this is a contemporary novel, a programme of wider reading
could include texts that help with the study of novels, such as
Jeremy Hawthorn's *Studying the Novel* (2005). Other texts such as
M. H. Abrams' *Glossary of Literary Terms* (1999) are invaluable for
the comprehensive definitions they give of commonly used literary
terms as well as explanations of aspects of literary theory.

Because of the centrality of the Second World War in *Atonement*,
it may also be worth considering comparisons with other novels
and films that also have this as a dominant subject matter. *Spies*
(2002) by Michael Frayn is a notable example of a novel that is set
in this period and films such as *Saving Private Ryan* (1998), which
focuses on the Normandy Landings, give a late twentieth-/early
twenty-first-century interpretation of this period. *Dunkirk* (1958),
which was directed by Leslie Norman and stars John Mills, depicts
the Dunkirk retreat and is, therefore, useful for a direct

comparative reading. Further to this, *Mrs Miniver* (1942) gives a propagandist's perspective of the effect of war in Home Counties England. Finally, *Casablanca* (1942) is one of many ill-fated war romances that have come to be thought of as classics.

With regard to the practice of adaptation, consider comparing other notable novel-to-film works. In his review of the film *Atonement*, Philip French points out the similarities with this and two other novels that have also been adapted: *The Go-Between* by L. P. Hartley and *The English Patient* (1992) by Michael Ondaatje (French, 2007, p. 18). These may be good starting points when making a comparative reading of the adaptation process.

In terms of the novel's structure and influences, increasing one's familiarity with the work of writers such as Virginia Woolf, Jane Austen and Henry James will mean that McEwan's literary allusions become more apparent. By following his reading, so to speak, readers will be more open to the references he makes and to the various styles he moulds as his own. *The Waves*, *Northanger Abbey* and *What Maisie Knew* are the respective novels that make useful starting points for this study.

For websites that give further information about the background to the Second World War and its origins, Spartacus Educational is a useful place to start and may be found at www.spartacus.schoolnet.co.uk/2WWbackground.htm. The historical context of the Second World War and particularly the evacuation from Dunkirk is explained with first-hand accounts on the BBC website. These narratives give the readers an insight into the atmosphere and conditions of this time and may be found at www.bbc.co.uk/ww2peopleswar/categories/c54696/.

Discussion questions

1. When studying this or any other text, it is vital to take into account the significance of the title, and in this case the suggested central importance of the concept of atoning for one's sins.

Does Briony make amends for the lie she tells? Is atonement ever possible for her? To be able to answer these questions, it is first necessary to consider the definition, and implications, of atonement and the difference between this and making reparations as Anita Brookner suggests in her review ('A Morbid Procedure').

2. Think of how McEwan explores the idea of the danger of the literary imagination and find some quotations from the text to support your points. Make references to instances in Part One where Briony prefers order over chaos and how this contrasts with Cecilia's outlook. It is also useful to note the places where Briony's imagination reconstructs events so that they become true in the narrative, such as when she lies about Robbie raping Lola.

3. Consider Briony's final revelation, where she explains the lovers did not meet and that this is her novel, and explain your reactions to this. Did you feel cheated, and/or did this add to your enjoyment? When answering this question, remember how this news alters the interpretation of the novel.

4. How does the structure affect the meaning of the novel? Examine and compare the style of the different main sections and avoid just thinking about the content. It will be necessary to bear in mind the different settings of parts One, Two and Three as well as the use (and non-use) of chapter divisions. To answer this as fully as possible, make note of how much of an impact the final revelation has on the readers' interpretation of the novel.

5. Find examples where *Atonement* refers to other works of literature

and discuss the influence these have on the narrative and your understanding of it. References to work by Virginia Woolf, D. H. Lawrence, Jane Austen, Henry James and T. S. Eliot have all been spotted in reviews, as well as many others; explain how, if at all, this literary signposting adds to the novel's depth.

6. Truth and lies are placed in the foreground of the novel, as when Briony lies about Robbie, and Cecilia and Robbie believe they know the 'truth' that Danny Hardman raped Lola. This is also a novel about secrets as Briony's atonement is connected to revealing the truth about what she did or did not see on the night she accuses Robbie. Consider how these references to lies, secrets and truth impinge on a reading of the novel and make it difficult to believe if or when Briony is telling the truth. To make more of this point, make references to 'London, 1999' and the use of the unreliable narrator.

7. Think about the relevance of the epigraph in relation to the rest of the novel. Remember that McEwan has called this his 'Jane Austen novel', at least with regard to Part One, and compare the way both *Atonement* and *Northanger Abbey* expound on how the literary imagination can manipulate narratives.

8. Compare the portrayal of war in the film and novel and explain how Part Two (in the novel) differs in terms of form and content to Part One (which is set in the Tallis country house in 1935). Think of the difficulties, if not impossibilities, of representing the past with good faith and explain if the novel is convincing in its depictions of the Dunkirk retreat.

It is also useful to consider the role of nursing during the war and in your analysis of Part Three consider the effect of this section playing such a large role in the novel. Is it possible to see this as balancing the narrative in that it gives space to the role of women as well as men?

9. How does this work compare to other McEwan novels? Look back to his earlier and later novels and note the similarities and differences between them. If relevant, explain how *Atonement* stands apart from the others.

10. Consider the way this work engages with morality and ethics and what effect the ambiguity of Briony's position as the supposed author has on the narrative. When responding to this point, bear in mind that it is not necessary for the readers to like or admire the narrator (or the author) to be compelled by the writing.

Works by Ian McEwan

Novels

Amsterdam (1998), London: Jonathan Cape.
Atonement (2001a), London: Jonathan Cape.
Black Dogs (1992), London: Jonathan Cape.
The Cement Garden (1978), London: Jonathan Cape.
The Child in Time (1987), London: Jonathan Cape.
The Comfort of Strangers (1981), London: Jonathan Cape.
The Daydreamer (1994), London: Jonathan Cape.
Enduring Love (1997), London: Jonathan Cape.
The Innocent (1990), London: Jonathan Cape.
On Chesil Beach (2007), London: Cape.
Saturday (2005), London: Jonathan Cape.

Selected other works by Ian McEwan

Other Fiction

First Love, Last Rites (1975/1991), London: Jonathan Cape.
For You: The Libretto for Michael Berkeley's Opera (2008), London: Vintage.

The Imitation Game: Three Plays for Television (1981), London: Jonathan
    Cape.
In Between the Sheets (1978), London: Jonathan Cape.
Or Shall We Die? (1983), London: Jonathan Cape.
The Ploughman's Lunch (1985), London: Methuen.
Soursweet (1988), London: Faber.

Non-fiction
'A Parallel Tradition' (2006a), *Guardian*, 1 April.
'An Inspiration, Yes. Did I Copy from Another Author? No' (2006b),
    Guardian, 27 November.
'Beyond Belief' (2001b), *Guardian*, 12 September.
'The Day of Judgement' (2008), *Guardian*, 31 May.
'How Could We Have Forgotten This Was Always Going to Happen?'
    (2005), *Guardian*, 8 July.
'Only Love and Then Oblivion' (2001c), *Guardian*, 15 September.

Film

Atonement (2007) (2008 DVD), dir. Joe Wright.
Being John Banville (2008), dir. Charlie McCarthy.

Interviews with Ian McEwan

Appleyard, Bryan (2007), 'The Ghost in My Family', *The Sunday Times*, 25
    March.
Deveney, Catherine (2005), 'First Love, Last Writes', *New Scotsman*, 30
    January.
Gerard, Jasper (2005), 'The Conversion of Mr Macabre', *The Sunday Times*,
    23 January.
Hamilton, Ian (1978), 'Points of Departure', *The New Review*, 5, 2, 9–21.

Kellaway, Kate (2001), 'At Home with His Worries', *Observer*, 16 September.

Lynn, David (2007), 'A Conversation with Ian McEwan', *The Kenyon Review*, 29, 3, 38–51.

Solomon, Deborah (2007), 'A Sinner's Tale', *The New York Times*, 2 December.

Sutherland, John (2002), 'Life Was Clearly Too Interesting in the War', *Guardian*, 3 January.

Selected works and criticisms

Andrews, Lucilla (1977), *No Time For Romance: An Autobiographical Account of a Few Moments in British and Personal History*. London: Harrap.

Banville, John (2005), 'A Day in the Life', *The New York Review of Books*, 26 May.

Bradshaw, Peter (2007), 'Atonement', *Guardian*, 7 September, p. 9.

Brookner, Anita (2001), 'A Morbid Procedure', *The Spectator*, 15 September, p. 44.

Calvino, Italo (1981), *If on a Winter's Night a Traveller* (1979), trans. from the Italian by William Weaver. London: Secker and Warburg.

Childs, Peter (2008), '*Atonement*: The Surface of Things', *Adaptation*, 1, 2, 151–2.

— (2005) *The Fiction of Ian McEwan*. London: Palgrave Macmillan.

Christopher, James (2007), 'Atonement', *The Times*, 29 August.

Cohen, Patricia (2008), 'An Author Enters the Fray', *The New York Times*, 24 June.

D'hoker, Elke (2006), 'Confession and *Atonement* in Contemporary Fiction: J. M. Coetzee, John Banville and Ian McEwan', *Critique: Studies in Contemporary Fiction*, Fall, 48 1, 31–43.

Dyer, Geoff (2001), 'Who's Afraid of Influence?', *Guardian*. 22 September.

Finney, Brian (2004), 'Briony's Stand Against Oblivion: The Making of Fiction in Ian McEwan's Atonement', *Journal of Modern Literature*, 27, 3, Winter, 68–82.

French, Philip (2007), 'Forgive Me, I Have Sinned', *Observer*, 9 September, pp. 18–19.

Gauthier, Tim S. (2006), *Narrative Desire and Historical Reparations: A. S. Byatt, Ian McEwan, Salman Rushdie*. New York and London: Routledge.

Haffenden, John (1985), *Novelists in Interview*. New York and London: Methuen.

Harold, James (2005), 'Narrative Engagement with *Atonement* and *The Blind Assassin*', *Philosophy and Literature*, April. 29, 1, 130–45.

Head, Dominic (2007), *Ian McEwan (Contemporary British Novelists)*. Manchester: Manchester University Press.

Hidalgo, Pilar (2005), 'Memory and Storytelling in Ian McEwan's *Atonement*', *Critique: Studies in Contemporary Fiction*, 46, 2, Winter, 82–91.

Ingersoll, Earl G. (2004), 'Intertextuality in L. P. Hartley's *The Go-Between* and Ian McEwan's *Atonement*', *Forum for Modern Language Studies*, July, 40, 3, 241–58.

Kakutani, Michiko (2002), 'Books of the Times; and when she was bad she was ...' *The New York Times*, 7 March.

Kemp, Peter (2001), '*Atonement* by Ian McEwan', *The Sunday Times*, 16 September.

Kermode, Frank (2001), 'Point of View', *London Review of Books*, 23, 19, 4 October.

Klein, Melanie (1937), 'Love, Guilt and Reparation', in Melanie Klein and Joan Riviere, *Love, Hate and Reparation*. London: Hogarth Press.

Lanchester, John (2002), 'The Dangers of Innocence', *The New York Review of Books*, 49, 6, 11 April, pp. 24–6.

Landesman, Cosmo (2007), '*Atonement* – The Sunday Times Review*', *The Sunday Times*, 9 September.

Lee, Hermione (2001), 'If Your Memory Serves You Well ...' *Observer*, 23 September.

Lyall, Sarah (1998), '*Amsterdam* by Ian McEwan Wins the Booker Prize', *The New York Times*, 28 October.

MacFarlane, Robert (2001), 'A Version of Events', *The Times Literary Supplement*, 28 September, p. 23.

McCrum, Robert (2005), 'The Story of His Life', *Observer*, 23 January, p. 5.

McFarlane, Brian (1996), *Novel to Film*. Oxford: Clarendon Press.

Malcolm, David (2002), *Understanding Ian McEwan*. South Carolina: University of South Carolina.

Messud, Claire (2002), 'The Beauty of the Conjuring', *Atlantic Monthly*, 289, 3, March, pp. 106–9.

Morrison, Jago (2003), *Contemporary Fiction*. London: Routledge.

Moss, Stephen (2001), 'The Literary Old Guard', *Guardian*, 6 August.

Mullan, John (2003a), 'Between the Lines', *Guardian*, 8 March, p. 31.

— (2003b), 'Looking Forward to the Past', *Guardian*, 15 March, p. 32.

— (2003c), 'Turning up the Heat', *Guardian*, 22 March, p. 32.

— (2003d), 'Beyond Fiction', *Guardian*, 29 March, p. 32.

Reynolds, Margaret and John Noakes (2002), *Ian McEwan: The Essential Guide*. London: Vintage.

Reynolds, Nigel (2006), 'The Borrowers: "Why McEwan is no Plagiarist"'. *Telegraph*, 7 December.

Rooney, Anne (2006), *York Notes on 'Atonement'*. London: Longman/Prentice Hall.

Ryan, Kiernan (1994), *Ian McEwan*. Plymouth: Northcote House.

Schemberg, Claudia (2004), *Achieving 'At-one-ment'*. Berne: Peter Lang.

Scott, A. O. (2007), 'Lies, Guilt, Stiff Upper Lips', *The New York Times*, 7 December.

Seaboyer, Judith (2005), 'Ian McEwan: Contemporary Realism and the Novel of Ideas', in James Acheson and Sarah C. E. Ross (eds), *The Contemporary British Novel*. Edinburgh: Edinburgh University Press, pp. 23–34.

Shone, Tom (2002), 'White Lies', *The New York Times*, 10 March.

Spivak, Gayatri Chakravorty (1988), 'Can the Subaltern Speak?' in Cary Nelson and Larry Grossberg (eds), *Marxism and the Interpretation of Culture*. Chicago: University of Illinois.

Swan, Robert (ed.) (2006), *AS/A-Level English Literature: 'Atonement'*. London: Philip Allan.

Tew, Philip (2004), *The Contemporary British Novel*. London: Continuum.

Tóibín, Colm (2007), 'Dissecting the Body', *London Review of Books*, 29, 8, 26 April, pp. 28–9.

Websites concerned with McEwan's work

www.ianmcewan.com, accessed 22 January 2009.

Mullan, John (2007), 'Profile: atoning for past sins', http://news.bbc.co.uk/
1/hi/magazine/6972320.stm, accessed 22 January 2009.

Kibble, Matthew (2000), 'McEwan, Ian', *Literature Online Biography*,
http://gateway.proquest.com/openurl?ctx_ver=Z39.88-2003&xri:pqil:res_
ver=0.2&res_id=xri:lion&rft_id=xri:lion:ft:ref:BIO002803:0, accessed
22 January 2009.

Matthews, Sean (2002), 'Ian McEwan', *British Council: Contemporary
Writers*, www.contemporarywriters.com/authors/?p=auth70, accessed
22 January 2009.

Websites for historical context

For more information about the background to the Second World War,
click on to Spartacus Educational at www.spartacus.schoolnet.co.uk/
2WWbackground.htm, accessed 22 January 2009.

The BBC website has personal testimonies of men who were at the evacuation at Dunkirk. These may be found at www.bbc.co.uk/ww2peoples
war/categories/c54696/, accessed 22 January 2009.

General literary studies

Abrams, M. H. (1999), *A Glossary of Literary Terms* (7th edn). Texas:
Harcourt Brace College.

Hawthorn, Jeremy (2005), *Studying the Novel* (5th edn). London: Hodder
Arnold.